POSITIVELY TEEN

A PRACTICAL GUIDE TO A MORE POSITIVE, MORE CONFIDENT YOU

NICOLA MORGAN

POPPY
Little, Brown and Company
New York Boston

Poppy
Hachette Book Group
1290 Avenue of the Americas, New York, NY 10104
Visit us at LBYR.com

Originally published in 2018 by The Watts Publishing Group in
Great Britain
First U.S. Edition: July 2019

Poppy is an imprint of Little, Brown and Company. The Poppy name
and logo are trademarks of Hachette Book Group, Inc.

The publisher is not responsible for websites (or their content) that are
not owned by the publisher.

Library of Congress Control Number: 2018952531

ISBNs: 978-0-316-52888-7 (hardcover), 978-0-316-52890-0 (pbk.),
978-0-316-52889-4 (ebook)

Printed in the United States of America

LSC-C

Hardcover: 10 9 8 7 6 5 4 3 2 1
Paperback: 10 9 8 7 6 5 4 3 2 1

★ Contents ★

A note from the author

I write a lot about adolescence, and visit tons of schools. Sometimes people ask me why. Why spend so many years of my life trying to help people a quarter of my age, who are younger than my own daughters? I could just say, "Because I care," but that doesn't explain *why* I care. Why do I care more about teenagers than any number of other things I could spend my life working for? I think it has to do with my memories of being a child and teenager and how I wish I'd known the stuff I talk about now. I could have avoided a lot of stress-related illness as a young adult and felt so much better about myself if I'd understood half of what I know today.

You see, from my earliest years I was fascinated by how things work. I used to take gadgets apart and try to put them back together again. I wanted to know exactly how they functioned, so that I could make them work better. Now, as an adult who has studied the brain and behavior, I realize that humans and our brains are really only machines, just super-complicated and extraordinary ones. The more we know about how we work, the better we can make ourselves. We don't know everything yet—maybe we never will—but we know a lot more than we did when I was young, and that knowledge is what I want to share with you in this book.

It's for you, from me.

Nicola

Introduction

Are you excited about being a teenager? Or worried? What expectations do you have: positive or negative ones? Parents and other adults can be very anxious about adolescence, as though they're expecting the worst. And the media often paints a negative picture, making it sound as though it's going to be *full* of stress. This book tries to avoid that. It aims to give you all the inspiring information you need to take control of your well-being as you approach or experience this powerful and important stage of your life.

Sure, there may be some difficult days or weeks—that's life, whatever age we are. You'll have exams; friendships might cause problems; your body is changing and you may be self-conscious about that; emotions can feel out of control, making you angry or sad; and you might want to do things that parents or teachers don't want you to do, which can create conflict. But there's so much to enjoy, too!

It's exciting to gain more control over your life and grow into the person you want to be—and find out who that person is. Being able to go out more independently—with friends or on your own—is fun and helps you learn important skills for managing your own life later on. Smartphones and social media give you huge opportunities to widen your knowledge and friendships, and modern technology also brings amazing chances to express yourself using video or blogs, with art, words, dance, and music. Your developing brain is allowing you to become an expert in whatever skills you spend time on, and you'll find that there are things you can do better than the adults around you.

Yes, you might make mistakes or a few wrong decisions along the way, but that's how we learn. And adolescence is about learning: learning to become independent, to do things for yourself, to have your own ideas, your own values, your own personal goals and successes. You might fail sometimes—in fact, you probably will—but failure is a step to success. If you try again, you have a better chance of succeeding, and your developing brain will help that happen.

Adults worry about failure and risks and sometimes try to prevent them by making things easier for you. But we don't learn things or become resilient by having people do everything for us: we learn by trying something for ourselves until we figure it out. If we succeed through our own efforts, we feel great about it. If we succeed because our parents did it all for us or told us what to do, it's not our own achievement. And it won't feel as good.

Adolescence is really about taking control of your life and your well-being. We have to grow from being a child (when we have very little control, because we don't know enough to have any) to being an adult (when we are supposed to have a lot of control over our own lives). As a teenager, you are developing the skills to acquire this control and independence, and that can't happen suddenly. *Positively Teen* helps you learn those skills by giving you practical advice about things you can do that will have a positive impact on your well-being, mood, health, and outlook. Many teens feel that they can't control anything: I aim to teach you that you can control far more than you think. It's what I wish I'd known when I was a teenager.

So, *Positively Teen* is based on understanding how your brain and body work, so you can be more in control. Not just through your teen years but through your whole life.

It will help you show adults that they can trust you, that you can learn to get things right, by aiming high and persevering. Your teen years can be full of success if you have the right attitude, tools, and knowledge. This book gives them to you.

Go for it! Be positively teen!

Well-being

You'll find the word "well-being" everywhere these days. It's a good word because it's easy to see what it means because of the "well" bit. But what does it mean *exactly*?

The best way to think about this is to see what's different about well-being compared to "happiness." You know what feeling happy is like. It's a positive feeling, the sort of emotion you might get if you were given a present you really wanted, or had done really well on a test or won a race or received some praise. It's a feeling you might get during a great vacation or when having fun with friends. So, we feel happy when something good happens. Sometimes when we have that feeling we don't quite know why. But we can't feel happy at the same time that we're feeling angry or sad, obviously. So, if we were feeling happy and then something bad happened, we would stop feeling happy. Instantly.

That's where well-being is different: if you have a good sense of well-being, and something sad or bad happens, you can still have good well-being. This is because well-being is not an emotion—not an immediate feeling. Well-being is a state of physical and mental health. You build it up over time, through lots of healthy behaviors (which this book will show you), and this gives you a reserve of mental and physical health. With a good state of well-being, you will still sometimes feel down or unwell—because everyone has those times—but you will also have a general feeling of "Yes, I'm OK; I feel pretty good a lot of the time; I can cope with what life throws at me today."

Well-being is strongly connected to "positive psychology." Psychology used to focus on problems; it tried to understand how humans work, so that psychologists could help fix our problems. But then along came positive psychology. This term was first used by Abraham Maslow, one of the world's most famous psychologists. It has become more popular with more recent scientists, such as Martin Seligman, who argued that psychology could be used to learn how to live well in the first place, and make problems less likely to happen. *Positively Teen* is a book that agrees! Positive psychology is about increasing our knowledge of how humans work and our self-understanding, so that we can have better control over our lives.

Of course, there are things in life that we can't control, and some people face many more challenges than others. If too many negative things happen, reserves of well-being can be worn away. But that makes it all the more important that we do what we can. And, luckily, most of the well-being advice is fun to follow!

FLOURISH

FLOURISH is an acronym I use to remember all the things we need to make our brain (and body) flourish, so we can have good well-being. Our brain is not just a 1.5 kilogram lump of wet, soft stuff inside our heads—though it is that, too! It is also responsible for everything we do and think, everything we fear and love and want, and everything we are. Looking after our brain is our most important task when caring about our well-being. All your thinking and feeling take place there. It's your "control center." In fact, you could say that your brain *is* you: it holds your personality and a whole bunch of unconscious things about you, as well as the things you choose to do.

HERE ARE THE EIGHT ELEMENTS OF FLOURISH

F is for FOOD—our brain needs fuel, just as the rest of our body does. In fact, the brain is a very fuel-hungry organ, using about 20 percent of the energy we take in. This energy comes from food, including most liquids (but not water on its own). You won't have enough energy to make your brain and body work well if you don't have enough food. You also need the right *sort* of food, and a good variety of it. Don't worry: you won't have to eat a lot of things you don't like! This is about finding things you *do* like.

L is for LIQUID—we need to take in enough liquids in addition to food. All drinks are made mostly of water, and that water content is essential. However, some drinks are better for us than others, and some are definitely not healthful.

O is for OXYGEN—oxygen is in the air we breathe, so we are obviously getting it just by inhaling. But some environments contain more oxygen than others, and there are some situations where we are not getting enough to feel and function well. There are simple ways to make sure you're getting enough.

U is for USE—different brain areas are used in different activities. The brain works on a "use it or lose it" principle. So, if you don't use certain areas, you will lose connections in those areas. For example, if you learn to play the piano, you'll grow lots of connections in certain areas, but if you then stop playing the piano, those connections will start to weaken and disappear, though usually not completely.

R is for RELAXATION—we can't keep working all the time; if we try to, our brain soon stops functioning properly. Stress chemicals build up and cause problems if we don't give ourselves breaks from pressure. Relaxation is not a luxury but an important part of our well-being. When we are really busy or going through a challenging period in our lives, remember this especially! Don't wait until you feel you "deserve" a break: allow for relaxing activities throughout that will help you work better in the end.

We need to choose these activities in an informed way, though. There are suggestions later in this book.

I is for INTEREST—our brains work best when we are interested in what we are doing. A brain chemical called dopamine is activated when something happens to excite or interest us, and this chemical helps us learn and process information. Some people call dopamine the "pleasure chemical," and it certainly corresponds to a feeling of excitement and pleasure. I call it the "yes" chemical because it makes us say "YES!" to things. It wakes the brain up and says, "LOOK! This is something worth paying attention to and going for!"

S is for SLEEP—scientists are discovering more and more fascinating things about sleep, including why it's so important, what it does to us, and how to get the best sleep we can. We know it has a huge effect on learning, mood, stress, and every aspect of our well-being. Luckily, now we know lots of ways to help ourselves get the right amount of sleep. Don't worry if you have bad nights every now and then—that's normal, especially at times of stress or excitement—but learn what you can do to give yourself more control over your sleep.

H is for Happiness—remember the difference between well-being and happiness? Well-being is more important, but having some experiences that make you feel actively *happy* is a valuable part of well-being. So, although there's no need to try to make every moment (or even every day) a happy one, it's important to have *enough* things in your life that make you happy.

But what if bad things are happening to you? If you're having a bad time, it becomes even more important to do some things that make you feel good, whether it's taking a relaxing bath, kicking a ball around, laying out in the sunshine in the park, or listening to your favorite music.

You'll find a lot of ways to incorporate **FLOURISH** into your life throughout this book. There are symbols to show you which of the **FLOURISH** elements each piece of advice is for.

You won't achieve all the **FLOURISH** elements every day, but the good news is that you don't need to! It's all about balance: you just need *enough* of each of them over the course of a week or so. Look for opportunities and get into the habit of thinking, "Oh, yes, I'll do that because it will help my brain in this way." The more you can do, the better.

It's all about doing your best to make good choices—choices that will help you feel and function better, choices that will give you a positive state of well-being and the best chance of flourishing, no matter what the day throws at you.

It's the key to being positively teen.

Your *Positively Teen* notebook

You will find a notebook useful and inspiring while you are reading *Positively Teen*. At various points, I will suggest writing something down. There are quizzes, for example, and other things you might want to make a note of. It can be a really good way to record your progress, achievements, and thoughts.

If you don't want to do this, you can just skip the parts where I suggest writing things down. If you don't have a notebook or you don't like your handwriting, you could use a computer or a tablet or even your phone. It's totally up to you.

Decorate your notebook however you like. It can be neat or messy. No one else has to see it, and no one is checking your spelling!

In the future, you'll look back on your teenage years and have a record of some of your thoughts. And you'll see how much you've changed.

POSITIVE BOOST boxes

Scattered through this book you'll see boxes containing **POSITIVE BOOSTS**. If it's possible, it would be great to stop your reading and do the suggested action right then. Or, if you can't do it easily at that moment, choose another one and do the first one later. For example, if you're reading in bed before going to sleep and the **POSITIVE BOOST** says, "Eat an apple" or "Call a friend for a chat," I am not suggesting you do it right away!

These boosts are there for three reasons: first, to give you ideas and remind you of the possibilities; second, to make sure you take breaks and vary your activity; and third, to increase your positivity and control. Build them into your life and use your imagination to invent others.

You could jot them down in your notebook and add your own favorite ideas. Do one whenever you like, not just when someone tells you to. It's your life.

More resources for you

You might want to find out more about some of the ideas I introduce in *Positively Teen*. So, I've put **Resources** at the end of each section, with relevant websites, books, and articles, so you can look them up quickly if you're interested. My website also has lots of resources for teenagers and their adults: *www. nicolamorgan.com*—and the Positively Teenage section has more specific things, including some items referred to in this book: *www.nicolamorgan.com/positively-teenage/*

When I mention research in the text, it's usually supported by a reference at the end of that section so you can investigate further. It's important to realize that a lot of research has to be done before we can be *sure* of something, and we have to use good judgment about whether to believe particular research. I have tried to include only claims that I am as sure as possible are true, and I've based them on the strongest science I can.

POSITIVE BOOST

Pour yourself a glass of still water.
Add any of these to it to make it more
interesting and tasty: a slice of lemon, lime, or
orange; some fresh mint; ice; a couple
of raspberries or blueberries. As you drink
it, feel its freshness and think about how
much good it's doing.

The FLOURISH quiz

Let's see how well you are taking care of your well-being before
you continue to read this book. It's time to do the **FLOURISH**
quiz! This quiz doesn't measure your well-being *exactly*, but
it gives you a sense of whether you are already making good
choices that will positively affect your mental and physical
health. It's a great idea to do it again when you finish the book.

Here's what to do:

Get out your notebook or a piece of paper or a laptop/tablet. (Don't write
in the book itself, because you'll need to do the same quiz again later.)

Look at each of the actions listed and base your response on the previous
twenty-four hours. If this has been a really unusual day, that doesn't
matter, but it's worth bearing in mind when you look at your score.

Score *one point* for each of the following actions that you have done
in the past twenty-four hours. Just one point, even if you did it twice.

Then add up the points to get your score. You'll see what each score
means afterward.

★ Quiz

The FLOURISH actions

 I spent at least half an hour doing something deliberately to relax.

 I kept attempting something I found difficult.

 I felt happy at some point in the day.

 I created something (in writing, dance, arts and crafts, woodwork, etc.).

 I took part in playing an instrument or I listened to music (actually listened, not just had it on in the background).

★ I exercised until I was out of breath (or went for a walk for at least thirty minutes).

 I spent half an hour reading for pleasure. (This can be *anything*, as long as it's something you want to read for pleasure, not because you have to. Reading on social media platforms or online forums doesn't count, but you can read an e-book if you like. If you really don't enjoy reading, you could spend this half hour drawing or doing a puzzle.)

 I turned my digital devices off for at least an hour before bed and didn't switch them on until I got up in the morning.

 I spent some time engaged in a hobby.

★ I did something kind for someone else.

★ I was engaged in something so deeply that I forgot the time.

★ I had at least eight hours' sleep.

★ I drank six glasses/cups of liquid. (Ideally, this should be water, but you may include some fruit/herbal teas, diluted juice, milk, or one glass of fresh fruit juice. A cup of coffee or ordinary tea counts as a half cup. Do not include soda or very sugary drinks, and obviously no alcohol.)

★ I ate at least five helpings of the following foods: fish, chicken, beans (including soybeans), lentils, nuts, oats, eggs, dairy products (e.g., yogurt or milk), seeded or whole-grain bread, any vegetables (including salad, hummus).

Your results:

12–14   Great! You are caring for your brain *really* well.

9–11   Well done—you are helping your brain.

6–8   You are doing some good things for your brain—but you could do even better.

3–5   Time to take control! Some simple changes will make a big difference.

0–2   Action needed! You only have one brain, and there's only one person who can look after it: you!

Try to score at least eleven points every day. Don't beat yourself up if you don't always manage it—it's a target, that's all—but the more times you succeed, the better. And great job if you do!

Once you've read this book, you'll be better equipped to have a great score and to maintain it throughout your teen years and beyond. It's the foundation of being positively teen. The rest of the book will help you do it easily.

Positively You

We are all the same because we are all human. But we are also all different from one another: each of us is literally unique. So, how does this work, and what does it mean? And what does understanding this have to do with your well-being?

I'll answer that last question first because it's quite simple: understanding ourselves is the beginning of being able to control our lives. The ancient Greeks had a motto, "Know yourself," and this is exactly what I mean. First, we need to know what being human is like, how we operate and feel, the basics of human psychology and behavior. If we know that, we can understand the idea that *I am behaving like this because this is how humans behave—it's normal.*

Second, we need to know how we *each* behave— the ways in which we are different from other people. If we know that, we can understand the idea that *I feel this or do this because I am this sort of person; this is part of me; I might be able to change some behaviors if I want to, but this is basically who I am.*

Let's look at what makes us the same

A human being is a species of animal. Humans share certain things: how our brains and bodies work, how we grow and develop, what we are capable of. If you think of other animals—cats or dolphins or eagles, for example—you'll be able to think of certain things or behaviors that make them cats, dolphins, or eagles: things that they each have or do that the others don't. Cats, humans, and dolphins share some characteristics—for example, they all breathe and they are all mammals—but we can tell a cat from a human or a dolphin. And even though there are lots of different sorts of cats, many of which look very different, we still know they are cats because of their long tails, fur, whiskers, paws, shape of their ears, and so on.

Perhaps the most important thing that makes humans stand out as different and "human" is the size of our brain and some of the powerful things we can do with it. One part of our brain is particularly large compared to that of other animals: the prefrontal cortex. If you touch your forehead, your prefrontal cortex is right there behind your skull.

The prefrontal cortex is often called the control center, and we certainly need it when we want control over actions, words, and decisions. But it's more than that. It's what we use for thinking about anything: figuring out problems, for example, or looking ahead to what might happen, based on our knowledge and understanding.

So, the power of our prefrontal cortex is one of the most important features of our being human. It's one way in which we are the same as one another, no matter where we live in the world, what color, gender, or age we are, or what religious beliefs we have; whether we're poor or rich, at peace or at war, bullies or victims, sick or healthy, kind or cruel, artist, athlete, nurse, scientist, teacher, salesperson, builder, or politician. We are all the same: human, with a human prefrontal cortex, human powers, human behavior, and human emotions. We all bleed; we all hurt. We should never forget that.

17

But we are also all individuals. There are no two people in the world who are *exactly* alike. Even identical twins, who begin from the same egg and share identical genes, are not exactly the same, though they may be *very* similar. If you look at the things that can make us turn out different, you'll see that some of them apply to identical twins, too.

Let's look at what makes us different

Different genes we inherited from our biological parents: "to inherit" means to take from a previous generation. We inherit genes from our parents—some from our biological mother and some from our biological father. If you have older or younger siblings, they will inherit a different combination of genes, so you might have some things that are the same and some that are different. If you have an identical sibling, your genes will be identical because you come from the same egg, fertilized by the same sperm.

Everything that has happened to us since the moment we were born: from huge life events, such as loss of loved ones or illness, to smaller things, such as hearing someone say something kind or cruel or being ignored or praised. (It's possible that things that happened while we were in our mother's womb might have made a difference, too, though we can't be sure what those differences are, and scientific understanding is still evolving about this.)

The values and ideas we learn from people around us: when we are children, we tend to absorb and agree with the views we hear from adults around us. So, if you are brought up with parents who hold particular opinions, you will probably share those views at first. As you go through adolescence, you may start to develop your own opinions, and they may be different in small or large ways.

The things we have spent time doing: each of us has spent different amounts of time on different activities. Some have learned a musical instrument or played tennis; others have spent lots of time climbing trees or riding horses or singing or acting or doing math problems or reading books. Everything we devote time to alters us a bit, changing our brain, knowledge, skills, and tastes.

Our age and stage of life: at different stages of life we will have different skills and knowledge, and different desires, responsibilities, needs, and priorities. A teenager has different things to think about compared to a small child who relies on his or her parents for everything; a new parent has different concerns as opposed to someone of the same age who doesn't have any children; people in their thirties will have different concerns from those who are just retiring.

Those are the *causes* of our differences, but what exactly *are* our differences? Let's look at some of the important ways in which you might be different from someone else. What makes you individual and unique? This is what you need to know, if you are to "know yourself" and be positively you.

POSITIVE BOOST

Make a poster of an inspirational quote that you like. You can find many online by searching "inspirational quotes." There are also lots of greetings cards that would work if you don't want to come up with something yourself. Choose a saying that reflects something you can believe in, something to hold on to and live your life by. Making a poster for your room will keep reminding you of this positive message.

Your teenage brain

Until the late 1990s, we didn't even know there was anything special about the teenage brain! Scientists thought it was just a bit more developed than a younger brain and a bit less developed than an adult brain. Now we know about fascinating changes that can help explain a lot about common teenage experiences.

It can be incredibly reassuring and empowering to understand that the changes you might experience and the feelings you might have are completely normal, and that many of them have a biological cause. If you do experience some of the more negative things I'm about to mention, try not to worry or blame yourself. Yes, you can certainly try to overcome them—and the more you try, the sooner you're likely to succeed— but these challenges are not your *fault*: there are some biological causes, in the form of hormone and brain changes, as well as more social causes, such as needing to fit in with your peers or dealing with routine pressures. Also, remember that this stage doesn't last forever. Whatever feelings or experiences you are going through are only temporary. That seems obvious, but it's easy to forget.

The main things to know about teenage brain changes

This is not just a human thing: adolescent rats and monkeys (and maybe other mammals, too) have some similar brain changes and behavior during puberty.

It's not modern: authors have written in negative ways about adolescents for hundreds of years. Shakespeare, for example, refers to your age group several times, listing various behaviors that sound like today's negative stereotypes. He even puts an age range on it: ten to twenty-three—and it turns out he was not far off! We know now that teenage brain changes start at around eleven (often a bit earlier, especially for girls) and don't finish until well into the twenties.

There are three stages of change: first, you grow many more connections between neurons (nerve cells, which carry messages around the brain and down the spinal cord). The peak age for this is around eleven for girls and twelve for boys. Next, you lose lots of connections. That sounds scary, but it's completely natural, and it's a very important stage. Think of it a bit like pruning a tree: if a gardener cuts back all the weak and scraggly branches, the tree will be stronger. Finally, starting at roughly fifteen or sixteen, the remaining connections get stronger still. They become covered with a substance called myelin that coats the connections and makes them better at sending messages.

The last brain area to become fully developed is the prefrontal cortex: I mentioned this earlier and described it as the "control center," but you might like to read about a few special things this brain area is known for:

✳ Controlling impulses and temptations

✳ Understanding emotions and controlling responses to them

✳ Understanding what someone else is feeling

✳ Judging whether something is a reasonable or risky thing to do and making the right decision about it

✳ Predicting the results of actions

A set of areas in the brain that *is* very well developed in teens is the limbic system, including the amygdala. This system is responsible for:

✳ Emotions—including anger, sadness, and fear

✳ Stress responses—"fight or flight"

✳ Instinctive reactions

✳ Impulse, temptation, and desire to do something

✳ Pleasure and reward

Teenagers have more brain activity than adults in areas that are active during situations of embarrassment (including those that are socially embarrassing, such as making a mistake in front of your friends). Adults often notice that teenagers seem super-embarrassed by something an adult wouldn't really care about. Well, it may be that you really *are* feeling more embarrassed.

Sleep patterns change:

1. You need more sleep than adults: about nine and a quarter hours a night on average, compared to eight hours for adults. (These are averages, and some people manage very well on less, while others seem to need more.)

2. Your "sleep hormone," melatonin, doesn't switch on until late at night—this is similar among adults—so it's not easy to fall asleep early.

3. Worse still, your melatonin levels don't switch *off* early in the morning, so you're likely to be sleepy at school.

Luckily, there are lots of things you can do to get more sleep. That comes under **Sleep well** in the POSITIVELY HEALTHY section on page 110.

★ Quiz

Let's take a look at how many teenage changes you're aware of in yourself. All of these are "normal" things to experience, but it's also normal *not* to experience all of them. People reach each stage in their own time and in different ways. Write all these things in your notebook. Check off the ones you've noticed in yourself, and write a comment or example next to it if you want to. (You'll find another version of this quiz on the positively teenage section of my website. It's completely anonymous, and I'd love for you to fill it in, as it furthers my research and helps me to help you!)

★ Feeling irritable and snappy

★ Feeling that parents and adults are not really on my side

★ Having more arguments with my parents than I used to have

★ Not being able to wake up easily in the morning

★ Not being able to get to sleep at night

★ Feeling sad or anxious much more than I used to experience

★ Being really self-conscious and embarrassed that people are looking at me

★ Doing things I know are a bad idea, because my friends are doing them

★ Thinking and daydreaming about boys or girls I'm attracted to a *lot*

★ Often wishing I could solve big problems in the world

Then write down any other things you notice about being the age you are. What are you feeling? What upsets or worries you? Or do you love everything or most things about the age you are in?

Based on that, what do you think are your big teenage issues? Would you like to see if your friends would do the quiz, too?

POSITIVELY YOU

A POSITIVE ATTITUDE

POSITIVELY HEALTHY

POSITIVELY BRAINY

POSITIVE ABOUT PEOPLE

A POSITIVE MOOD

Resources

TEEN BRAINS

My book aimed directly at young people:
Blame My Brain—The Amazing Teenage Brain Revealed

Two sites with lots of references to the science behind teenage brain differences: *www.pbs.org/wgbh/pages/frontline/shows/teenbrain/*

and *teenmentalhealth.org/learn/the-teen-brain-2/*

Shakespeare's comment from *The Winter's Tale*, Act III, Scene 3:

"I would there were no age between ten and three and twenty, or that youth would sleep out the rest; for there is nothing in the between but getting wenches with child, wronging the ancientry, stealing, fighting...."

National Sleep Foundation webpages for teens: *sleepfoundation.org/sleep-topics/teens-and-sleep*

Research on the impact of smartphones on children's sleeping patterns: *jamanetwork.com/journals/jamapediatrics/article-abstract/2571467*

Research on how rats' sleeping patterns change with age: *www.journalsleep.org/Articles/220202.pdf*

Your teenage body

So, what else makes teenagers different? Our bodies change throughout our life. Your body will change a lot between the age of ten and the end of adolescence. You've almost certainly heard about this at school, from your parents, and from magazines. Also, depending on your age, you'll have noticed these changes yourself.

This isn't a book about puberty, so I'm not going to go into the details. I've referenced some websites on page 29 that will answer any questions you might have about something you've noticed happening to your body. What I want to do instead is help you have a positive attitude about your body as it changes.

There are three things you should know. Reminding yourself of these facts will help you a great deal.

1. Everyone is different.

2. What you see on the Internet and in magazines is often fake.

3. Most people have something they don't like about their body.

Let's explore these three points now.

1. Everyone is different. Some bodies change a lot and quickly; others don't change as much, and do so slowly. Try not to compare yourself to the people around you, although I know this can be difficult. What your body is doing says nothing about the person you are.

Some people are excited and positive about their body changes. It's easier to feel like this if you are developing at the same rate as most of your friends—an "average" rate. But if you are developing earlier than your friends, you might feel more self-conscious or negative about it. You might even try to hide your changes so people don't notice them. Please don't feel you have to do this: it's going to be such a short time before your friends catch up. Just be proud of leading the way!

Or you might be developing later, and that can be upsetting, too, as you probably want to be just like your friends. Both boys and girls can be embarrassed by not developing the outward signs of physical maturity. But some teenagers develop more slowly or later than others. It's not a race or a competition: it's just that everyone's body is naturally different. It is very rare for this to be caused by a medical problem, but if you are worried, it's worth seeing a doctor for reassurance (or investigation if you are one of those rare cases).

Of course, those questioning or uncomfortable with their gender may have extra difficulties here. Now would be the time to get expert advice if you haven't already. See the **Resources** panel on page 29.

2. What you see on the Internet and in magazines is often fake. Photos and videos showing models and actors (and even vloggers and other video-makers) are often "enhanced" and "perfected" in some way. Even your friends' photos on social media have usually been selected as the ONE photo out of dozens or hundreds of selfies that they didn't like.

If you don't keep reminding yourself of this, it can be a real cause of low self-esteem. To be honest, it's better to look at those pictures and videos as little as possible. Or, if you do look, remind yourself (often) that the person looks that way because of professional makeup that has taken hours, clever lighting, and photo-enhancing software to airbrush out wrinkles or rolls or curves and, often, to make someone look far thinner than they really are.

When these people don't have those advantages, or they've just woken up in the morning, they look like everyone else.

3. Most people, especially in wealthier societies with a big consumer culture, have something they don't like about their body. Even the people you think have a fantastic body/face/hair/whatever. This is the saddest thing about the whole issue: too many people are going around dissatisfied with something trivial about their physical appearance. A fortune is spent on breast enhancements or reductions, nose-straightening or nose-reducing, whitening teeth, or changing the color of skin.

Let me tell you something I only remembered as I was writing this book: I used to hate my nose. I thought it was way too big. I didn't do anything about it, thank goodness, and at some point it became such a nonissue that I literally forgot about it until now. I looked in the mirror after writing that, just to check, and found myself thinking, "Really? What was that all about?"

Does this mean we should just ignore our bodies and faces and not take care of them? No, I don't think so. There are natural and important ways to have strong, healthy bodies, face, skin, and hair, which I'll get to in the POSITIVELY HEALTHY section on page 74. It's right to take care of those things, and it's completely fine if we want to emphasize the parts we like best and downplay the parts we don't like. We might change

POSITIVELY YOU

A POSITIVE ATTITUDE

POSITIVELY HEALTHY

POSITIVELY BRAINY

POSITIVE ABOUT PEOPLE

A POSITIVE MOOD

hairstyles, choose certain clothes, or pick a few products that might help. But we need to keep everything in perspective. Too much effort, worry, or money spent on changing how we look is only going to lead to more unhappiness and stop us from focusing on important ways to make the most out of life. Concentrating on negatives prevents us from enjoying or even noticing the positives, and that's a real shame.

Of course, if you have a condition that affects your appearance, or something noticeable that is causing you major problems in your life, it's understandable that you might want a medical solution if there is one. If you have something like this and it's upsetting you, talk to a doctor and tell them how you feel.

But when I talk about being unhappy about your appearance, I'm referring to the range of natural body changes that take place during adolescence. I want to encourage you to feel either good or at least OK about them, however quickly or slowly they are happening.

We are all different; none of us is as perfect as a professional photo; and there are more important things to think about than whether our breasts or nose or muscles or size or voice or hair is "perfect." If you look for perfection, you'll never find it. And what is perfection, anyway?

You are you; you are changing all the time; how your body is now is not how it will be next month or next year. Just be healthy and try to forget the rest, or at least let it occupy the smallest amount of your headspace as possible.

You'll find lots of tips about living well and looking after your body in POSITIVELY HEALTHY on page 74.

Resources

For more information about teenage health and well-being:

Agnes—the life guide for girls. I think this is an awesome site, and I wish I could find something similar for boys: *agnesforgirls.com/*

Kids Health: *kidshealth.org/en/teens*

TEENAGE BODY CHANGES

Aimed at girls: *www.girlshealth.gov/body/index.html*
Aimed at boys: *www.youngmenshealthsite.org*

BODY IMAGE

A great YouTube video with a message on body image and media: *www.youtube.com/watch?v=24Xa1Nw8eJY*

PBS on raising a girl with a positive body image: *www.pbs.org/parents/parenting/raising-girls/body-image-identity /raising-a-girl-with-a-positive-body-image/*

Kids Health for teenagers: *kidshealth.org/en/teens/body-image.html*

Kids Health for parents: *kidshealth.org/en/parents/body-image.html*

Information on eating disorders: *https://www.nationaleatingdisorders .org/body-image-0*

GENDER-IDENTITY QUESTIONS

Learn about the gender spectrum: *https://www.genderspectrum.org /quick-links/understanding-gender*

And especially for teenagers: *https://www.genderspectrum.org /explore-topics/teens*

Know and value your "character strengths"

Schools tend to focus on measuring skills that are an obvious part of the curriculum. I don't blame schools: it's what they have to do.

But we need many other abilities in order to do well in life. Some of these are called "character strengths" and are important for overall well-being. They also affect general performance and success, partly because well-being helps you succeed, but also because these strengths include things like "perseverance," which obviously affect the quality of your work. There are ways to measure these strengths, as you'll see, and each person has different character strengths.

The particular strengths I'll refer to are the twenty-four character strengths listed by the VIA Institute on Character. They have been well researched: more than five million people have taken the survey, and there's an enormous amount of information on their website (see page 35) that wil allow you to find out more.

Here are the twenty-four character strengths in alphabetical order. With permission from the VIA Institute, I have adapted the descriptions for this book, adding questions to help you think about the meaning of each one.

Appreciation of Beauty and Excellence—do you get a buzz from seeing something you think is beautiful? Do you feel admiration when you see something that required real skill?

Bravery—how willing are you to try things you might fail at? Do you try out for teams even though you might not be selected or might not excel? Do you stand up for your opinions even if others disagree?

Creativity—do you spend time on art, music, photography, writing, or a hobby involving making things? Do you have creative ideas and imagination? Do you tend to have unusual approaches to problems?

Curiosity—are you eager to investigate and discover new things? Do you like new experiences? Do you want to know how things work?

Fairness—how important are fairness and justice to you? Do you feel angry when you see someone being treated unfairly or when you yourself have been treated unfairly? If there was a rule you thought was unfair, would you fight to have it changed?

Forgiveness—can you "move on" after someone has apologized (or even if they haven't)? Or do you hold grudges and think differently of the person who has wronged you, even after the incident has blown over?

Gratitude—do you feel and show gratitude for good things in your life? Are you aware of the good things, and are you able to remember them when something bad happens?

Honesty—are you true to yourself, or do you pretend to be who you aren't? Do you value sincerity, truthfulness, and honesty?

POSITIVELY YOU

A POSITIVE ATTITUDE

POSITIVELY HEALTHY

POSITIVELY BRAINY

POSITIVE ABOUT PEOPLE

A POSITIVE MOOD

Hope—how optimistic are you about life? Do you expect good things to happen to you? If you imagine your future, is it bright? Do you describe yourself as a mostly lucky person?

Humility—when you've achieved something great, are you able to not boast about it? Are you a modest person, capable of praising other people's achievements?

Humor—are you often playful and lighthearted? Do you tend to see the lighter side of a situation and find humor even when things are difficult?

Judgment—are you good at critical thinking—able to think through all sides of an argument and not jump to conclusions?

Kindness—do you enjoy doing things for others? Do you make sacrifices for other people?

Leadership—do you like organizing other people to get things done? Do you find you can positively influence others to help them to work toward a goal?

Love—are you able to love, and to accept when someone loves you? Is it important to you to be close to others and to genuinely like them?

Love of Learning—do you like practicing new skills and topics, becoming an expert at them and adding to your overall knowledge? Do you enjoy learning new facts and gaining greater understanding?

Perspective (you might also call this wisdom)—do you often manage to come to a sensible and logical conclusion about things rather than acting on pure emotion? Can you think about and discuss moral issues and see other people's points of view, so that you can find a solution that isn't just about what you want?

Perseverance—if you don't succeed the first time, are you strong and resilient enough to try again? Can you think of something you've kept trying even though it didn't work out the first few times?

Prudence—are you careful and thoughtful about your choices and actions? Are you able to be cautious when necessary and avoid too much risk?

Self-regulation—do you have good self-control, and are you able to stop yourself from doing something you shouldn't do? When you feel angry, are you able to control it well?

Social intelligence (you might call this empathy)—how in tune are you with others? Do you care what others are feeling? Do you often try to help when someone is feeling bad? How aware are you that other people may think and feel things differently from you?

Spirituality—do you have a spiritual side? Do you have faith in a higher meaning or a religion that you feel connected to and that gives you comfort?

Teamwork—is it important to you to work well in a team? Do you think society needs people like you who are socially responsible and think of others? Are you a loyal person, and do you value supporting other people? Would you call yourself a good citizen in your family, your school, your groups, or the wider community?

Zest—how much energy do you usually feel? Do you approach most activities in a positive, excited way? If you're about to try something new or tackle a problem, do you dive in with enthusiasm and a "can do" approach?

(Character strengths © copyright 2004–2018, VIA Institute on Character. All rights reserved. Used with permission. www.viacharacter.org.)

POSITIVELY YOU

A POSITIVE ATTITUDE

POSITIVELY HEALTHY

POSITIVELY BRAINY

POSITIVE ABOUT PEOPLE

A POSITIVE MOOD

★ Assess your character strengths

The only way to get an accurate picture of your character strengths is to do the survey on the VIA website. But if you can't do that now, or prefer not to, here are ways to think about these strengths in relation to your own life. You could also do this activity and *then* do the actual survey and see whether you were right! Use your *Positively Teen* notebook to record your answers.

 Write down the four or five strengths you *believe* you would score best on.

 Write down the three to five strengths you believe you would score least well on.

★ Can you think of one or two reasons or examples of why you chose each particular strength?

★ For your strongest ones, can you think of one action to perform in the next few days that would develop them further?

★ For your weakest ones, think about whether you would like to improve these strengths. If there is one that you really don't care about, cross it out. For the ones you do care about, can you think of one action to perform in the next few days that would make them stronger?

Write them as goals: things you plan to do. Make your goals clear, achievable, and easy to measure. (You might want to look at **Set the right goals** in A POSITIVE ATTITUDE on page 60.)

You can build a positive attitude and grow your self-esteem if you find ways to exercise your main strengths even more *and* do simple things to boost your lesser ones. These are not fixed skills: you can improve them if you want to. Just keep them in mind and look out for opportunities to do so. (You'll also find a use for them in **Notice what went well** in A POSITIVE ATTITUDE on page 70.)

POSITIVE BOOST

Write a thank-you note or card to someone who has done something kind to you or whose support you appreciate. It could be a text message or it could be a homemade card to your sister or dad or teacher or friend. You'll feel good, and so will they— a double win!

Resources

CHARACTER STRENGTHS

For the free survey that lets you measure your character strengths: *www.viacharacter.org/www/Character-Strengths/VIA-Classification* Look for the VIA Youth survey for people aged ten to seventeen. (Note that you have to register your email address, so check with an adult about whether you are allowed to do this.)

For research into the role of character strengths: *www.viacharacter.org/www/Research/Character-Research-Findings*

Your different personality

and the need for quiet

Another thing that makes us each different is our personality. Some people are anxious and easily stressed; some are really ambitious, while others are more content with smaller goals; some are leaders and others have no desire to lead; some like working in teams and others prefer to do things on their own. People differ in how selfish, vain, optimistic, or patient they are.

It's good to acknowledge personality differences and try not to compare ourselves to someone else. Of course, there are some behaviors we might like to change—doing selfish things, for example, is not something to be proud of. There's no such thing as a perfect personality, but a positive approach would be to say to yourself: "If I behave in a way I don't like, I can change that behavior, though it might be difficult. I can change negative behavior while still keeping my personality."

There is one personality difference that seriously affects our sense of well-being. I won't suggest you change it—you probably can't. But if you understand it, you can take steps toward approaching it positively. Let's look at introversion and extroversion.

Introvert or extrovert?

You might think introversion is about shyness, and extroversion is about liveliness. They're not. Introverts and extroverts can both be shy or lively. Rather, these character traits are about how our bodies and brains react to social situations and how we spend or gain energy from those situations.

Social situations include everything from a super-relaxed chat with your best friend to walking into a crowded dining hall where you don't know anyone. They include collaborative work, making a speech, and answering questions in class—anything where you interact directly with other people.

Introverts

Introverts usually react more strongly in social situations, often feeling more stressed and becoming more tired. They can handle them perfectly well (though they may need to practice their skills and get used to the situation), and, in fact, introverts can be great at public speaking and making conversation because they are very sensitive to the audience and work hard to please. But introverts will use more energy to cope and therefore be more tired after these situations.

School is *full* of such situations! In fact, the only time when you're not in a social situation during a school day is when you're working on your own. The rest of the time, as an introvert, you're spending energy and becoming exhausted dealing with a barrage of social situations. That's not good for your well-being and performance.

Extroverts

Similarly, if you are more of an extrovert, you *need* these social situations—otherwise you might get bored, frustrated,

POSITIVELY YOU

A POSITIVE ATTITUDE

POSITIVELY HEALTHY

POSITIVELY BRAINY

POSITIVE ABOUT PEOPLE

A POSITIVE MOOD

uninterested, or disengaged. Extroverts feel energized after social interaction and thrive on being around other people. You'll get enough of both during a school day, but you may need to seek social activities on weekends.

★ The introvert/extrovert quiz

Though you may already have a good idea, you might want to know for sure where you stand on the introvert/extrovert scale. There are free quizzes online (with links on the *Positively Teenage* website), but for now here are six statements. The more strongly you agree with them, the more likely you are to skew toward the introverted end of the scale:

★ I often think, "I really need to be on my own for a bit."

★ I get tired after talking to friends for a long time, and I feel better after a break.

★ I like chatting to just a couple of friends more than being with a larger group.

★ I prefer quiet places to noisy, busy ones.

★ I find my mind becomes overloaded when I'm with other people, and the noise can be stressful. I often make excuses to leave.

★ I much prefer working on my own to doing shared work.

Positive strategies to work with your introvert or extrovert needs

Accept and value your personality, however introverted or extroverted you might be. Each trait has advantages, and all are equally valuable. Remember that most people are a bit of a mixture, and here are some possible advantages of each:

✳ Both can be great friends: introverts listen well and are sensitive to the needs of others; extroverts can raise the mood of the people around them and inject fun into a group.

✳ Both can be really good public speakers: introverts are likely to think carefully about what the audience wants and respond to feedback; extroverts tend to be less self-conscious and bring a natural energy to a performance, often finding it easy to make people laugh.

✳ Both can be excellent leaders: introverts can make the rest of the team feel heard and respected; extroverts may carry difficult ideas or decisions through more easily.

✳ Both can be equally creative: introverts tend to come up with their best ideas alone, while extroverts do better in a group.

Encourage your teachers to investigate and understand these personality traits because they are bound to have both introverts and extroverts in every class, and different activities suit different learners. Point them toward the **Resources** on page 41. Some teachers may need to adapt their teaching style to work equally well with both personality types. Much schoolwork is collaborative nowadays, and teachers need to be attuned to the fact that not everyone loves working in pairs or groups.

If you are very introverted, think of ways to get enough peace and quiet to feel refreshed and ready to work. It's important not to run away from social interaction, but you need enough quiet time, too. Talk to your school librarian, as the library can be a good place to get away and enjoy a time-out. Every school should provide a place, time, and permission to chill out—where people are not required to be social when they don't want to be.

Whether you're more extroverted or introverted, be clear about your needs. If you want a time-out during break or lunch, or on weekends, explain to friends that you are absolutely fine but you just want a bit of time to regain your energy or do

POSITIVELY YOU

A POSITIVE ATTITUDE

POSITIVELY HEALTHY

POSITIVELY BRAINY

POSITIVE ABOUT PEOPLE

A POSITIVE MOOD

some thinking. Make sure people realize you are perfectly fine, so they don't come and bother you. When you get home from school, if you want to be alone for a while, say so.

Similarly, if you're pretty extroverted and you're desperate for more social outlets, look for others who'd like to get together; have a spontaneous party, picnic, or trip to the movies on the weekend; or join a drama club or any other group-based activity. Just tell people openly that you're someone who needs lots of social activity, but you understand that not everyone else does.

Share this knowledge about introversion and extroversion with your friends. Many of them will be grateful to understand themselves better, too! You could all have some fun doing an online quiz to "measure" your introversion/extroversion and start to value one another's skills.

Be brave and tackle things you find difficult. Extroverts need to learn to be on their own sometimes, and introverts have to try to be social and perform in front of others. Those are skills we need in life, and they make us feel good. So, don't run away from them. Whatever you need help with, ask for it. No matter what we are trying to do, it's usually easier to take small steps and get used to difficult things gradually.

POSITIVE BOOST

Make a sign to go on your bedroom door that tells your family if you want to be alone. Use a positive message, such as "Thinker at work—peace needed" or "I love you all but this is me-time" or "Silent zone—I'm working," or whatever is appropriate. Explain to your family that when the sign is up, they should respect it.

Resources

INTROVERSION AND EXTROVERSION

A book aimed at young people, parents, and schools, which focuses especially on being an introvert at school: *Quiet Power* by Susan Cain

The Quiet Revolution website, with advice and stories for introverts and extroverts on how to appreciate our quiet side: *www.quietrev.com/*

A nice interview with Susan Cain, aimed at parents of introverted teenagers, but I think interesting for young people as well: *http://yourteenmag.com/family-life/communication/susan-cain -introverted-teenager*

An article on being a sensitive extrovert: *www.psychologytoday .com/blog/sense-and-sensitivity/201408/how-cope-highly -sensitive-extrovert*
It's a small piece but very useful because it avoids the trap of thinking that introversion is all about shyness: yes, you can be both extroverted and sensitive.

FEELING SHY
A couple of reassuring looks at shyness and social phobia:

WebMD: *https://teens.webmd.com/teen-social-phobia#1*

Kids Health: *http://kidshealth.org/en/teens/shy-tips.html*

Different lives

Different people experience easier or harder situations. I don't think anyone can go through life without any hurdles. Would you want that? I wouldn't. I'd feel uncomfortable to be so lucky! The things that make us proud are those times when we manage to overcome obstacles and challenges. They may have been tough at the time, but looking back, we can be proud of how we coped.

Some challenges are huge, more than we can manage on our own. Others seem big at first but turn out to be more manageable than expected. Often, worrying is worse than the actual problem. Other situations are more minor. Some are temporary and others permanent.

I don't want to focus too much on these problems—this is a book about positives, not negatives—but I think we should remember that everyone has something going on that affects how easy it is to develop well-being. It won't make it impossible—you can have good well-being even when bad things happen—but it makes a difference. And acknowledging this is a positive start. If you are going through a rough patch, don't be too self-critical. Ask for help when you need it, and go easy on yourself.

Things that make lives different

Money—for many families, money is a big worry. Money problems can affect the health and well-being of the adults you live with, and also impact your own life.

Family—every family is different. Try not to compare yours to others, because you only know your own experience—other families can seem perfect when they aren't. There's no rule that says what sort of family works best, either. So whether you have one parent, or two, or more; whether you have siblings or not—none of that predicts how well your family will work.

Illness—either affecting you or someone you love. This includes mental illness, of course.

Disability—a whole range of possible challenges.

Gender—if you are uncomfortable with your gender or questioning the way you've been brought up, or you're being pushed in one direction or another by people around you, this will make your preoccupations different from those of someone who isn't thinking about these things.

Sexuality—at some point, you will probably find yourself attracted sexually to someone. This could be simple or complicated, depending on whom you're attracted to and the reactions of people around you.

Religion and culture—during adolescence you might start questioning the religion or culture you've been brought up in. Also, the cultural and religious rules you follow may be different from those of your friends.

Random events—your family could go through any number of difficult events. Even relatively ordinary things like changing houses or schools can affect you and your family.

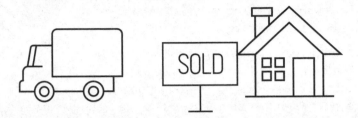

Childhood history—some people have a difficult start in life. There are various reasons why this can happen. Being a parent is not easy, and some parents struggle more than others.

There are lots of smaller things, too. If you think about it, every family is made up of individuals with different personalities. So, every family and every home is going to be different. You have the one you've got, until you leave and make your own home. Then you can do things differently or the same—it will be up to you!

Summing up

You've seen lots of ways in which you are an individual—features that make you, you. You've discovered special differences in teenage brains and looked positively at your adolescent body changes. You've gained real insight into your own valuable character strengths and thought about ways to develop them further. Your introverted and extroverted features make more sense to you now, and you've seen how to value your individual personality.

Thinking about some of the many possible differences between people's lives has helped you see yourself in context, too. Understanding and recognizing all these human differences will help you as you navigate your own adolescence. You are on your way to being able to tackle any challenges positively and sail through the years ahead.

Now let's look at making the most of those differences and creating some real paths to lifelong success.

A Positive Attitude

Looking after ourselves begins with the right attitude. Otherwise, we won't even bother to try. This section takes a look at some ways of thinking that will make a positive difference to your life now, through adolescence and beyond.

First, what exactly is a "thought"? It feels like a vague, invisible idea that floats through your head. It doesn't feel like a physical thing. But a thought *is* a physical thing. It's the result of an electrical signal passing through pathways between the neurons in your brain, often at high speed. (The speed varies, depending on things like which networks are involved, but five hundred feet per second is average.)

Next, realize that each time you have the same thought, it follows the same network of pathways between the neurons.

Now understand that each time you use that network, you make those pathways stronger. You know how when you walk through snow, and then walk along the same route several times, you make that path more obvious, stronger, and easier to follow each time? That's what happens in your brain when you think or do the same thing over and over again.

I'll talk about this again when I talk about the power of practicing things. But, for the moment, just think about the fact that each time you have the same thought, you make it easier to have that thought again because you have made the pathways stronger. (On the Positively Teenage page of my website, you'll find a link to a neat presentation that demonstrates this idea of pathways.)

Your thought could be a positive one or a negative one. It could be "I did well on that test" or "I'm bad at science." It could be "If I work hard, I can pass that test" or "I'm not as smart as the rest of my class." It could be "I'm really glad I met Lucy" or "People don't like me." By having that thought, you make it more likely you'll have it again. And if you think it over and over again, you make a physical path in your brain that allows that thought to keep coming.

Finally, realize that this means that if you have negative thoughts over and over again, you are creating physical pathways in your brain—pathways of negative thinking.

Have you heard of "brainwashing"? You might have read a book in which someone has been "brainwashed." It sometimes shows up in science fiction or thrillers, where villains change the thoughts of their victims so they think the way the villains want them to. Brainwashing happens: it's what we do to ourselves every time we keep having repeated thoughts, whether positive or negative. And you have more control over that than you think.

This is why people so often talk about the need to think positive thoughts. And it's why athletes and other performers are encouraged to picture themselves succeeding. Imagining is just the same as thinking: it makes a pathway in our brain.

POSITIVELY YO

A POSITIVE ATTITUDE

POSITIVELY HEALTHY   POSITIVELY

POSITIVELY BRAINY

POSITIVE ABOUT PEOPLE

A POSITIVE MOOD

Focus on what you can control

A positive attitude begins with being able to focus on what we can control and ignore what we can't. It's sometimes very difficult to do, and I admit, I often struggle! But being able to do this as much as possible is a crucial part of well-being.

Do you often worry about things you can't control; things that probably won't happen; things that have already happened and that it's way too late to change; events happening in the news; things about your appearance that you don't like? Do thoughts like this sometimes keep you awake at night? Or stop you from concentrating on things you're supposed to be concentrating on? Welcome to the world of the worrier!

It's quite natural, but it's not pleasant or useful. In fact, it's sometimes the opposite of useful because it takes time away from the things you could be usefully thinking about. There are things worth worrying about, but they should be the right things at the right time.

So what's worth worrying about, and what isn't?

Let's break it down into types of worrying, and think about whether they are worth spending time on or not. (Of course, if something bad has happened, it's normal and healthy to feel negative for a while, but I'm talking about spending time thinking about the *wrong* worries.) Do you spend your time thinking about…

…things that have already happened, that you had no control over? (For example, you didn't get picked for the team or school play because, even though you did your best, someone else was better, or you didn't feel well and couldn't do your best.)

→ *Totally out of your control: try not to dwell on these worries. Of course, it's normal to feel upset, but stop thinking about it as soon as you can. Look ahead to the next opportunity.*

…things that have happened, that might have gone differently if you'd done something else? (For example, you didn't do as well as you should have on a test.)

→ *You can't change the past, but you can figure out if there is something you can do differently next time. Once you've worked that out, move on.*

…things that have happened, which you can't change, but there's something you can do to improve the situation or feel better? (For example, you and your friend had a bad argument.)

→ *Again, you can't change the fact that it happened, but if there's something that could help now (such as an apology), work out what it is, decide when you can do it, and then don't give it another thought.*

…things that might happen in the next few days or weeks? (For example, you might not get picked for a school team, or a boy/girl you like might not ask you out.)

→ *How important is it? How much is it in your control? Is there anything you can do about it? If not, stop thinking about it. If there is, work out what action you can reasonably take and then stop thinking about it. Only think about it when it's time to act.*

...very bad things that might happen one day? (For example, someone you love being seriously ill or dying.)

> *It's fine to spend a few moments thinking about how you'd cope if something awful happened, but then you need to try to push it away. It's natural to worry when a disaster is reported on the news, too, and it's a good idea to talk to an adult about your fears. But try not to let it take over your thoughts. Dwelling on possible but very unlikely disasters is not useful, and can make you suffer more than necessary.*

...negative thoughts about yourself? (For example, anything negative about your personality, appearance, life, friendships, or abilities.)

> *Don't spend time worrying about these things. Read the POSITIVELY YOU section again. You're changing all the time and seeing yourself through negative eyes. If it falls into the category of "things I can't control," push it away. If you think you can control it, ask yourself whether you should have to. And if you shouldn't, dismiss it.*

...good things that might happen? (For example, you might win lots of money or a national competition.)

> *It's fun to daydream about things like that. Go for it! Some people might argue that it's a waste of time, but it's good to think positive thoughts and be optimistic. Don't let it stop you from actually doing the work that successful lives usually need, though. There's interesting research that suggests positive daydreaming can be really useful and good for concentration. I'll talk about that in **Just think** on page 196.*

There is one particular time when you should definitely push bad thoughts and worries away—when you're trying to sleep. If you're losing sleep over negative thoughts, take a look at the advice about sleep on page 110, where you'll find specific suggestions for dealing with intrusive worries.

Do you procrastinate? The syllable "cras" in "procrastination" is Latin for "tomorrow," and "putting things off until tomorrow" is a common habit. Is there something you know you should be doing now? It could be as small as taking glasses downstairs from your bedroom or writing a thank-you note for a birthday present. The answer is really simple: just do it. NOW! You'll feel so much better when you've gotten it off your mind.

★ You and control

In your notebook, draw a vertical line down the middle of the page. Write the heading **A lot of control** on the left, and **Little or no control** on the right. Then look at the seven things on the list below and think about how much control you usually feel you have over each of them. Write each item in the appropriate column, according to your personal feelings. Don't turn the page until you've finished.

★ Food and drink

★ Genes and early childhood

★ Exercise

★ Sleep

★ Mood and feelings

★ Things that happen to me

★ Stress

Now turn the page.

Did your answers look like this?

★ A lot of control	★ Little or no control
Food and drink	Genes and early childhood
Exercise	Sleep
	Stress
	Things that happen to me
	Mood and feelings

That would be a common response from teens who don't feel they have much control over their lives. Apart from "genes and early childhood," which obviously you can't control at all, there's no absolute right or wrong answer here, and we could discuss why you *might* put the others in either column. But this book is all about helping you reach this arrangement:

★ A lot of control	★ Little or no control
Food and drink	Genes and early childhood
Exercise	Things that happen to me
Sleep	
Stress	
Mood and feelings	

Sleep, stress, mood, and feelings are all things you can have a lot of control over.

Focus on the present: mindfulness

Let's look at tricks to help you focus your thoughts in healthy, positive ways on what you can control. Mindfulness is one good way to manage negative thinking. It's also calming and can be great for reducing stress in busy, noisy lives.

Some schools encourage mindfulness, and many people of all ages find it very helpful. But people should not think it is the answer to all of today's problems. It doesn't work for everyone, so if it doesn't work for you, there's nothing wrong with you! Also, for a few people it can make mental conditions worse, so classes should be conducted by people with appropriate training. But if you're just trying to press pause on your busy mind, then it's a good thing to practice.

What is it?

Mindfulness is a type of meditation. It encourages you to focus on the present, on thoughts and feelings and senses. You can't do mindfulness while rushing around or while people are talking to you. And you can't do it while you're on social media, either! You have to devote your whole headspace to whatever it is that you are doing and feeling at that moment.

During mindfulness practice, when a negative thought comes into your mind, you don't have to push it away. You just let it in and let it pass through your mind without trying to stop it or criticizing yourself for having it. This is helpful for people who find it hard to push negative thoughts away.

How can you bring mindfulness into your life?

Although you do need an expert teacher to learn mindfulness properly, you can still practice mindful thinking and actions without taking special lessons. Here are two examples:

✳ Take something you're eating or drinking. Focus on it closely: notice the textures, the smells, the colors, the tastes. Notice what it feels like in your mouth, how it slips down your throat, the taste it leaves behind. Derive every possible thought and description you can from it. Give that piece of food your entire attention for a minute.

✳ Just sit or lie in a comfortable place and listen. Listen to the sounds in your room, then draw your attention to sounds farther away. Can you hear traffic? The wind? Distant voices? Electricity humming in the air? A clock ticking? A fly? Buzzing? Humming? Clicking? Swishing? Just think about them all, maybe describing them in your head.

By focusing on these simple sensations or experiences, you can calm your thoughts and push away the sense of not being in control. You have learned to control your mind and your body, and given it a break from your noisy head. You've learned that you can—at least some of the time, when you choose—control your thoughts.

Resources

<u>MINDFULNESS</u>

Mindfulness for teens has some excellent resources and free apps: *mindfulnessforteens.com/resources/resources-for-mindfulness/*

AnxietyBC explains mindfulness and offers ideas: *youth.anxietybc .com/mindfulness-exercises*

POSITIVELY YOU

A POSITIVE ATTITUDE

POSITIVELY HEALTHY

POSITIVELY BRAINY

POSITIVE ABOUT PEOPLE

A POSITIVE MOOD

Into the future—
lucky or not lucky?

We can control some parts of the future but not others. We can control whether the next words we speak are kind, for example. We can control whether to raise a hand to answer a question when we know the answer (though this is harder for some people than others). But we can't control whether it's going to rain next Saturday or whether we'll find some money on the street next week. We can't control our luck.

Or can we? Well, there's evidence it's sometimes possible. This is all about optimism versus pessimism. An optimist expects good things to happen, but a pessimist expects the worst. Of course, sometimes one of them is right and sometimes the other is right, but is it possible that how we think about the future can in some ways actually affect the future?

The psychologist Richard Wiseman, in his book *The Luck Factor*, talks about his research on the different behaviors of people who describe themselves as particularly lucky or unlucky. For one experiment, he picked Martin, who described himself as lucky, and Brenda, who thought of herself as unlucky, and set up a situation where they were asked to come separately to a café for a meeting.

The research team set this up cleverly. First, just outside the door, they left some money on the pavement. Second, they arranged the tables with an actor at each, pretending to be a customer. One of these actors played the part of a successful businessman. When Martin arrived, he saw the money and picked it up, sat next to the businessman, and got into a conversation with him. When Brenda arrived, she didn't notice the money and, although she sat next to the same "businessman," she didn't start a conversation. Later, when asked about their day, Martin described in great detail the interesting conversation and finding the money; Brenda didn't really have much to say about the day.

Now, this was just two people, and there are many reasons why they might have behaved differently, but the point is that they had the same chances but approached them and engaged with them differently. Wiseman's book contains many such stories.

You're more likely to be "lucky" and find money if you keep your eyes open, and you're more likely to make useful connections if you connect with people, aren't you?

So, maybe there are things we *can* do to control our "luck" a bit: being curious and observant, being eager to join in and try something, saying yes to opportunities, being positive. These things could help. Do you know the phrase "You need

POSITIVELY YOU

A POSITIVE ATTITUDE

POSITIVELY HEALTHY

POSITIVELY BRAINY

POSITIVE ABOUT PEOPLE

A POSITIVE MOOD

to be in it to win it"? In other words, if you don't try, you can't win.

But don't blame yourself when bad things do happen! You didn't "fail" just because you had some bad luck. Also, don't set your goals too high, expecting everything good to happen all the time; otherwise you might often be disappointed.

Instead, try to grow a sense of "I'm going to approach this (day or semester or competition or exam or whatever) positively. I'm going to be open to opportunities because then there's a really good chance of things going my way. But if they don't, never mind—next time could be better."

Resources

LUCK AND OPTIMISM

The Luck Factor by Richard Wiseman: research involving people who consider themselves lucky or unlucky. I recommend *The Luck Factor*. It's very readable and offers strategies and tips. Although aimed at adults, it's very accessible to younger people.

Here is the story of one of his experiments: *http://news.bbc.co.uk/1 /hi/magazine/3335275.stm*

★ Quiz

Write your answers in your notebook or on a piece of paper or a laptop:

★ How quickly can you think of three good things that have happened to you in the last year? (Big things or small things—whatever comes to mind.)

★ How quickly can you think of three bad things that have happened to you in the last year? (Again, big or small.)

★ Which of the above questions was easier to answer? (This gives an indication as to whether you are more optimistic or pessimistic. Of course, if some unusually bad/good things have happened to you recently, this might affect your response.)

★ How likely do you think it is that something good will happen to you tomorrow or next week? Very likely/somewhat likely/don't know/somewhat unlikely/very unlikely.

★ Write down three good things that might happen tomorrow or next week.

★ Write down three things you would like to achieve in the near future. (It could be this week or this semester.)

★ Think about the three things you would like to achieve in the near future. What do you think are your chances of succeeding? (If you think your chances are 90 to 100 percent on all of them, change two of them to more challenging ones! It would be good to have a range of difficulty: one where you might easily fail, one where you have a very good chance of succeeding, and one somewhere in the middle.)

For each of your goals for the near future, write down:

★ How much will success be owing to luck and how much will it be up to you?

★ Any things you will need to do if you are to have the best chance of succeeding.

★ How you will feel if you succeed.

Now look at your answers and think about one final question:

★ Do you feel as though you have a lot of control over whether good things will happen to you in the next month?

Set the right goals

That point about optimism leads straight into this: we need to set goals that are just right, so we can approach the future positively and so we can succeed often enough.

If we always set goals that are too difficult, we will probably fail too often. We might even start to expect failure, and too much failure risks lowering self-esteem and well-being. There's something psychologists call "learned helplessness." This means that if people continually experience being "helpless"—either because they keep failing or because other people always do things for them and they never get the chance to succeed by themselves—they stop trying. It's like a cycle of weakness. If you have the chance to succeed by yourself, you learn what you can do, more than what you can't. And then you can set the bar a little higher each time.

If we set goals that are always too easy, we won't feel really satisfied and proud of ourselves. Also, it's important to fail *sometimes*, because it helps us become resilient. Resilience is about learning to deal with difficulty and grow stronger. I'll talk about this in more detail on page 63.

SMART goal-setting

SMART stands for these things (though in some explanations the wording differs slightly):

Specific—goals shouldn't be vague. They should be things like: "Finish my homework by 9 PM" rather than "Work harder."

Measurable—you need to know when you've achieved your goal: "Finish my homework by 9 PM" is measurable, while "Work harder" isn't.

Achievable—don't set goals you know you can't achieve.

Relevant—there needs to be a point to what you want to do, even if only you know what it is! For example, your goal might be to spot twenty different makes of car by tomorrow. If that's relevant to you and your love of cars, go for it!

Time-limited—you need a cutoff for your goal. "I will work harder" isn't time-limited, but "I will work hard for an hour" is.

If you think about all those New Year's resolutions that people break, you'll see they're often goals such as "I will lose weight," "I will drink more water," "I will stop procrastinating," or "I will exercise more." These resolutions break the SMART rules, so they are hard to keep.

Think about the goals you set for yourself, whether they are small ones such as "I will focus really well for one hour and not look at my phone," or bigger ones such as "I will practice the violin four times a week so that by the end of this semester, I will be good enough to move to the next level." Set targets that will make you proud if you achieve them. And change your goals if necessary: if you discover you've been expecting too much of yourself, go easy; if you think you can do better, raise the bar a little.

POSITIVELY YOU

A POSITIVE ATTITUDE

POSITIVELY HEALTHY

POSITIVELY BRAINY

POSITIVE ABOUT PEOPLE

A POSITIVE MOOD

POSITIVE BOOST

Write a goal down. Unless it's private, write it in big letters on a card to put above your bed or desk. Decorate it. The more effort you put into it, the more important it will feel to you. Make sure it is something that you can measure and has an end to it. If you achieve your goal, cover it with exclamation marks and stars!

Resources

GOAL SETTING

Kids Health has good general advice about goal-setting:
http://kidshealth.org/en/teens/goals-tips.html

The Teen Compass has excellent practical advice and downloadable goal-setting sheets:
www.theteencompass.org/explore/smart-goals-defined

Build resilience

Resilience is the ability to bounce back after a negative event. That could be something like failing a test, or it could be a sad or scary incident. It could be small or big. Setbacks happen to us at various points in our lives. They are unpleasant at the time, but they are useful because they allow us to develop resilience and to value the good times.

People used to think resilience was like a personality trait—something you had either a lot or a little of, something you were born with and couldn't control. But psychologists now say resilience doesn't work like that: it's something we *can* grow.

Resilience is certainly a good thing to have— a way of thinking that allows us to say: "OK, so that happened. I didn't like it, but I can survive it and I'll be all right. In fact, I'll be stronger in the end." It allows us not to beat ourselves up about mistakes we've made or things people have said to us, and permits us to not keep dwelling on situations that were bad at the time but that are done and over with.

How can you become more resilient?

It's useful to repeat certain positive thoughts, building strong pathways in your brain. Here are some examples, which you can use whenever a relevant situation happens:

★ How I feel now is not how I will feel later—this will pass.

★ It's normal to feel sad/angry/scared now, but this will pass.

★ There is someone out there to help me if I need it, and it is not a sign of weakness to ask for help.

★ This will make me stronger.

★ I will be proud of my progress. Even if I take some steps backward, I will be proud of my steps forward.

★ I can take small steps, but I will get there in the end.

★ The past is the past; I can control lots of parts of the future.

★ Many people have dealt with things like this—or worse.

★ I have friends who will be happy to help me with this.

★ There will be many good moments ahead in my life.

This whole book aims to help you be more resilient by giving you practical tools to develop positively and to take things in stride. Just believing that you can have more control over your reactions to what happens will help build resilience.

Resources

RESILIENCE

Two useful webpages with resilience advice:

Child and Youth Health: www.cyh.com/HealthTopics/HealthTopicDetails.aspx?p=243&np=293&id=2198

American Psychological Association: www.apa.org/helpcenter/bounce.aspx

Build a "growth mind-set"

According to psychologist Carol Dweck, there are two ways of thinking that affect our attitude toward failure and success and how pessimistic or optimistic we are, and those things can affect our chances of success. They are called "fixed mind-set" and "growth mind-set." (A mind-set is a way of thinking, attitude, or set of beliefs.) Let's see which one you have and then I'll explain what it means. Read the following two paragraphs and see which one you agree with more strongly.

VS

POSITIVELY YOU

A POSITIVE ATTITUDE

POSITIVELY HEALTHY

POSITIVELY BRAINY

POSITIVE ABOUT PEOPLE

A POSITIVE MOOD

1. "I believe we are born with certain skills and talents. The things I'm good or bad at now are mainly because of what I've inherited from my parents or just how my brain and body work. By now, my skills are mostly fixed, and I'll always find certain subjects easier than others. So, the most sensible strategy is just to go with that and not waste time expecting to get better at things I'm no good at. It's too late to change! After all, Mozart was a child genius and composed his first symphony at age six and his father was a talented musician, too, so it's obvious we inherit these skills or are just lucky to be born with them. Skills and talents are mostly things we're born with—practice and teaching just develop them further."

2. "I believe skills and talents are things we develop and have very little to do with genes inherited from our parents. If someone is better than me at sports or music or math or reading, it's because they've spent more time than I have on those things at an early age. Maybe their parents made them practice so they became an expert at it. So, that means that I can become better at anything I want to, if I spend more time practicing whatever it is. After all, Mozart was exceptional because he was trained by his father from a very early age and spent a lot of time practicing. He threw himself into his music, and that's why he was so successful at such a young age. Skills and talents mostly grow through practice and teaching."

★ If you identify mostly with the first one, that suggests you have a fixed mind-set. You believe that what you're good at is mostly a question of luck because it's about what you were born with and other things you can't control. So, you believe that you can't *become* good at something if you don't have the right natural talents in the first place.

★ If you identify mostly with the second, you have a growth mind-set. You believe that if someone is better at something than someone else, it's mostly because of the amount of time they've spent on it, practicing and getting good teaching, often at an early age.

You probably sometimes have one mind-set and sometimes the other, by the way. You might generally believe that you can get better with practice, but sometimes find yourself thinking, "I'll never be able to do this—I'm just not made that way." It's normal to experience both types of thinking.

You have to be a bit realistic, too. You've probably already spent many years acquiring some skills more than others. So, you might have really strong soccer or piano-playing or math or artistic skills because you've already spent time on them. And you might have spent less time on other things, so those skills aren't as strong.

The point is that we need to stop thinking, "I'm bad at this" or "She's better than me at that," and we have to think instead, "I can be better at this if I persevere" or "She's only better than me because she's spent more time on it—I can change that by practicing."

It turns out that there are some things we've been forgetting or ignoring about Wolfgang Amadeus Mozart, too. His father was a professional music teacher and composer. His older sister had music lessons, and Wolfgang seemed to love music at a very early age. (Lots of toddlers are like that, especially with parents who encourage them!) So, from the age of about three, Wolfgang sat in on his sister's lessons, and he began studying as soon as possible. Again, with a supportive father, this would happen easily. Also, his parents lost five other children, so a huge amount of attention would have been showered on Wolfgang and his sister. From the earliest age, he lived and breathed music, learning with the best teachers and performing regularly.

We are told that he started composing at the age of five, but what does that mean? His father's handwriting is on his early works, so it's not clear what the boy did himself. His father made money from his children's performances, so we might guess that he exaggerated when he billed them both as "child prodigies." Mozart was certainly an exceptionally brilliant musician—quite possibly the best the world has ever seen—but everything in his life points toward his enjoying the best environment in which his skills could flourish: good teaching, plenty of encouragement, and lots and lots of practice. There is no proof that he was "born like that."

Now that we know so much more about how learning and expertise develop, it's more likely that, even if there were such a thing as "natural talent" or the "genes for genius," without many hours of practice and good teaching, this natural talent wouldn't appear.

So, think yourself into a growth mind-set by focusing on the idea that perseverance and hard work are good ways to predict success. And you'll feel much prouder if you've achieved it by yourself rather than having it given to you by a fairy godmother when you were a baby!

Resources

FIXED AND GROWTH MIND-SETS

Carol Dweck's work:
http://big-change.org/growth-mindset-research-2/ and *https://www.mindsetworks.com/science/*

Matthew Syed, author of *Bounce*:
www.matthewsyed.co.uk/2015/09/16/the-power-of-learning-from-your-mistakes/

Syed's TED talk encouraging people to acknowledge failure and confront mistakes: *https://www.youtube.com/watch?v=MmVCYqs3mko*

Malcolm Gladwell's book *Outliers* popularized the idea that ten thousand hours of practice are needed to become an expert at a complex task, such as violin playing. This article explains his view: *http://wisdomgroup.com/blog/10000-hours-of-practice/*

Gladwell based his idea on research by Professor Anders Ericsson, but Ericsson has distanced himself from Gladwell's conclusions, as this article explains. Ten thousand hours was offered by Ericsson as an average, varying greatly between people and between tasks. Many other factors are important, such as determination, good teaching, and also the type of practice. Ericsson says it's not the quantity but the quality of practice that matters most: *www.makeuseof.com/tag/10000-hour-rule-wrong-really-master-skill/*

Notice what went well

This is a brilliant strategy for a positive attitude from the world of positive psychology and is based on strong research. (You'll find references to it in the **Resources** on page 72.) It addresses the problem of our spending too much time thinking about what went wrong. If we do this too often, we spiral into negativity and anxiety and miss opportunities to be optimistic and in control.

One thing, though: it's also perfectly healthy to think about "what went wrong." That's how we can try to make sure it doesn't happen again, if there's something we can do differently. So, I'm not saying you shouldn't think about those things, too. Just make sure you spend *more* time thinking about what went *right*.

Here's how to do it. Set aside a few minutes before you go to bed each night and do the simple things in the box on the next page. Lots of research, notably by Martin Seligman and his colleagues, shows that this simple daily act can have an enormous positive effect on many aspects of well-being and health. And it's a great way to relax before going to sleep.

⭐ What went well?

Identify three good things that happened today. They can be big things, such as doing well on a test or winning a game. Or they can be really small, such as having your favorite food at lunch or sitting in the park with the sun on your back.

Then say why each one happened. It could be that you did well on a test because you worked hard. It could be that you had your favorite food at lunch because you got lucky today.

Finally, say which of your character strengths you used. (See **Know and value your "character strengths"** on page 30.) Did you use Perseverance or Bravery? Hope or Gratitude? Love of Learning or Creativity? You probably used a combination. Acknowledge them!

But what if you have something really difficult happening in your life?

I'm afraid bad things happen to good people just as often as to bad people, and there's no doubt that some events can be really hard to deal with. Whatever life has thrown at you and your family, you can't change the past. So, try to leave it where it is: behind you. And focus on some things you *can* do. Here are a few tips:

✳ If it's a new situation, realize that time is a great healer—it's a cliché, but it is true! That's not saying you'll "get over it," just that your feelings will change and the pain will fade.

✳ If it's a long-term situation, you will be able to find a "new normal," even if it takes time.

✳ If it's something you can't control, spend as little time as possible thinking about it, especially when you're trying to go to sleep.

✳ Build positive things into your life, small activities that give you a break from the bad stuff. Like sunshine in winter.

✳ Even with difficult stuff going on, you're allowed to laugh! Laughter is very good medicine. It releases endorphins— chemicals in the brain that are often called "happy chemicals"— and you feel more upbeat.

✳ If you find your situation really hard, talk to a trusted adult. Teachers are a good place to start because they are trained in how to respond. They might not have the answers themselves, but they know how to help you find them. Counselors are specially trained to help you process your thoughts in a healthy way.

✳ Use this book to understand how to have control and develop a growth mind-set: huge tasks can be managed if we take them one step at a time. Every long journey begins with one step; our talents are not gifts we're born with but things we develop through practice. So, be determined and you can handle anything life throws at you. And then you will feel proud— and rightly so!

Resources

WHAT WENT WELL

Research about the effectiveness of focusing on what went well comes from psychologists led by Martin Seligman. His "Three Blessings" exercise is here, along with an exercise called a "Gratitude Visit": *www.brainpickings.org/2014/02/18/martin-seligman-gratitude -visit-three-blessings/*

Seligman also talks about this on Action for Happiness, which has excellent resources: *http://www.actionforhappiness.org/take-action /find-three-good-things-each-day*

An article by Seligman for the BBC where he explains the science behind this: *news.bbc.co.uk/1/hi/programmes/happiness_formula /4903464.stm*

Summing up

Attitude is one of those things you might have thought you couldn't control. In this section you've learned that you positively can!

We began with ways you can control negative thoughts, thinking about which ones are useful and which are not, and seeing whether you can calm anxiety and your busy brain with mindfulness techniques.

You've thought about how perhaps an optimistic attitude can affect your luck. You've learned how to set sensible goals that will help you toward success, and how to value the things that have gone well for you.

More important, by understanding that it's grit and determination more than talent and luck that bring success, you've given yourself a growth mind-set instead of a fixed one.

These are big ideas, but they're also simple and well researched. They will help you approach your teenage years with excitement, curiosity, and positivity.

Positively Healthy

If we want to have good mental and physical well-being, an important part of that is looking after our bodies. The choices we make about food, drink, exercise, fresh air, and sleep all make big differences in how well we feel and how well our bodies work for us.

When you were a young child, your parents or caregivers made all these decisions for you and you didn't have very much choice, but now you can start taking control of these things.

There are so many ways of giving yourself the best chance of staying healthy, and that's what this section is all about. I hope you'll find it really empowering, too, as you learn the facts you need to make the best choices. It's your body and your life!

Eat well

The great news is that you don't have to eat things you don't like! Eating well doesn't necessarily involve dieting, and it's not boring, pointless, expensive, or difficult. It takes a bit of knowledge (coming up) and a bit of thinking (you can do that), and then you'll be set up with habits to help you be as healthy as possible, for life.

Another good thing is that it's an area of your life where you can very easily take control. And whoever does all the food shopping and cooking in your house will probably welcome your getting involved in the choices. Making good choices about food is one way you can approach your teen years positively and strongly.

We don't have to make perfect choices every time, and there's nothing wrong with eating something junky every now and then. It's about information and balance. It's about knowing how to fill your body with enough fantastic, tasty food that you get all the nutrients you need. If you do that, you'll help your brain, mental health, physical health, learning, mood, skin, eyes, teeth, digestion, and energy levels. Just with food!

What happens if you make right or wrong choices?

When it comes to food choices, there are long-term effects and more immediate ones. It's hard to be very enthusiastic about long-term ones because they are so vague and distant: "lowering your risk of cancer and other illnesses," "having stronger bones," or "being healthier" may be excellent goals, but it's difficult to stay motivated when you can't see quick results.

Let's focus on one effect that you can notice immediately: how you feel. Good food choices make a noticeable difference in how you feel for the rest of the day. They affect energy and concentration, mood and emotional and physical feelings. If you eat a sugary snack, for example, it gives you a burst of energy, but within minutes that energy is spent and you're hungry again, and maybe dizzy and snappy. Your concentration suffers, and so does your mood. But make a different choice— yogurt with granola or a banana on top; a tuna, egg, or chicken sandwich; a bowl of oatmeal; a handful of nuts—and you'll have energy and concentration for far longer. This section is all about making these choices.

So, what are the super-brain foods?

There is no one magic food that makes brains and bodies work best. We need a wide number of nutrients—the "useful" parts of foods that nourish us—and no single food contains all of them. It's true that some contain more nutrients than others, and I'll get to those in a minute, but I just want to say now: don't pay too much attention to headlines saying that Brazil nuts/blueberries/oatmeal are the "answer" to having a brilliant mind. They are part of the answer, as you'll see, but only a part. (And don't worry if you don't like Brazil nuts, blueberries, or oatmeal, because there are other options!)

Another reason for not concerning yourself too much with anything claiming to be a "super-food for the brain" is that there's the temptation to consume lots of it, and that's never a good idea: if you eat huge quantities of one thing, you won't be able to eat enough of other things. It's all about balance. Also, just because something is good for us, or necessary, doesn't mean that a *lot* of it will be even better than a "normal" amount. Overeating even the healthiest foods can cause problems.

There are three main things to think about:

1. Eating enough

2. Having lots of variety

3. Making enough positive choices

1. EATING ENOUGH

We need to eat enough because our bodies and brains can't work when we don't. Food gives us energy, and our bodies and brains use—or "burn"—that energy for everything we do. This includes not just physical things like running and swimming but mental things like reading, writing, and figuring out problems, and automatic things like breathing, regulating temperature, and reacting to stress. We also need energy for growing and repairing cells, and we use it while sleeping, too. Even if we lie in bed all day, we use energy, but actively using our bodies and brains means we use more.

That energy comes from calories—nowhere else. So, you need enough calories. If you don't get enough, obviously you'll lose weight, but you may also slow the natural processes that keep your body healthy. So, if you need to lose weight, you should do this slowly and under medical supervision, to make sure you're not harming yourself.

POSITIVELY YOU

A POSITIVE ATTITUDE

POSITIVELY HEALTHY

POSITIVELY BRAINY

POSITIVE ABOUT PEOPLE

A POSITIVE MOOD

How many calories should you consume?

Don't count calories! Let me explain.

First, the only people who should count calories are those who've been put on a "calorie-controlled" diet by a qualified medical expert. In that case, you'll be told how many calories you need. And how much a person needs depends on height; other aspects of size, such as bone size or build; gender; age; and level of exercise. So I can't say how many calories you need because I don't know those things about you. But not having enough calories can cause you harm.

Second, counting calories can lead to an obsessive attitude about food, and that isn't healthy. I don't want you to control food intake like that: it's painful, negative, and unhelpful because not all calories behave in the same way. Calories from some foods are processed and turned into energy quickly, while calories from other foods take longer to be processed. So, looking at the calorie content of something is not enough to tell you whether you're making a healthy choice.

How do you know if you're eating enough?

If you're a healthy weight, you're probably eating enough. You can find out whether you are a healthy weight or not by looking at an online chart for your height and age. This usually measures your "BMI" (body mass index), and there's a different ideal range for different genders and ages. Take a look at the links in the **Resources** on page 86.

What if you're hungry all the time? Does that mean you're not eating enough? Well, it might. Or it might be that you're not making the best choices, because some foods (processed sugary ones, for example) turn into energy so fast that the energy is quickly used up and you're soon hungry again.

What if your weight is too high? Does that mean you're eating *too much*? Well, it might. Or it might be that, again, you're not making the best choices.

If you're worrying whether you might be eating too much or too little, ask an adult with medical training, such as a school nurse or your doctor. If you're just wondering but not worrying, I suggest you follow the advice below (**Having lots of variety** and **Making enough positive choices**) because if you're doing those things, and you're within healthy weight guidelines for your age and height, and you have enough energy for daily life, you're probably eating the right amount.

I'm emphasizing eating *enough* because some people your age restrict their food in the hope of getting thinner. That's not how to have a healthy body and brain, and certainly not how to be positively teen! Being healthy means eating an amount of food that keeps the body and brain working well. While you're growing, you need more food to fuel that growth.

Also, sometimes young people who feel they are too tall think that if they eat less they won't grow so much: but height is mostly controlled by genes and things that happened during your very early years, so you can't change that now. Restricting your food now just risks your not having the nutrients for good skin, nails, eyes, hair, digestion, and all the other things your body needs.

2. HAVING LOTS OF VARIETY
Eating a rainbow

One of the best ways to have variety is to eat a "rainbow" of foods—those in lots of different colors. (This does *not* mean Smarties or M&Ms or other foods that are artificially colored!) Think of all the different colors in these foods: strawberries, bananas, red and green grapes, carrots, tomatoes, corn, peas, oranges, cucumber, yogurt. The colors are produced by different nutrients, so it's simple to choose a natural variety without needing to know what's in each food. And if you don't like the suggestions in that list, there are so many other things you can choose. Just look for foods that are colored by nature.

All the food groups

Another way to get variety is to make sure you select from different food groups. You don't need to have every group at every meal—though it's good to aim for that—but over a day you want a good balance of them all. There are five main groups, and farther down you'll see lots of examples of where to find each one:

* Fruits and vegetables: containing many vitamins, as well as fiber to fill us up and help digestion.

* Other carbohydrates: important for quick energy. (Fruit and vegetables are mostly carbs, too, but this group consists of things like rice, pasta and bread.)

* Protein: important for growing and rebuilding cells, but also a great carrier of energy and longer-lasting than many carbs; keeps hunger away for longer.

* Dairy: usually from cows, but all animal milk products are dairy. Dairy contains protein and important vitamins and minerals, such as calcium, that are essential for strong bones. Your calcium intake as a teenager is important later in life. If you have a health reason for restricting dairy, you still need these nutrients, so get expert advice about alternatives.

* Fats: as a rule, the important fats are found in plants and oily fish. They are an essential part of our diet, partly because they help us absorb other nutrients.

If there's any food you can't eat for medical reasons, don't worry: there are always other ways to get the goodness you need. Or if you're vegetarian, vegan, or anyone else who avoids certain foods, get advice about how to eat well. You'll find **Resources** about food on page 86.

3. MAKING ENOUGH POSITIVE CHOICES

It's best not to think about "good foods" and "bad foods" because then you can start feeling guilty, which is unnecessary. Think about "foods I should have plenty of" and "foods I should only have occasionally." The main trick is to find enough foods that you *like* in that first category. Then you'll fill yourself up on them.

Foods to have plenty of:

Fruits and vegetables

✳ Any fruits and vegetables! Especially vegetables, as they're less sweet.

✳ Some vegetables to try: broccoli, spinach, lettuce, carrots, beets, peas, corn, beans of any sort, sweet potatoes.

✳ Some fruits to consider especially: berries (blueberries and black currants are fantastic), tomatoes, apples, bananas—all of these contain good quantities of a variety of essential nutrients.

Protein-rich foods

✳ Fish—any fish, but especially tuna, mackerel, salmon, and herring

✳ Chicken—go easy on deep-fried chicken, and avoid chicken (or other meat) that has been "processed" in a factory into pies and sausages, and sliced meat that has been "re-formed." But roast chicken, stir-fry, or baked chicken breasts or thighs are all good.

✳ Beans, lentils, tofu, soy—these are really important parts of our diet, but especially so for vegetarians and vegans.

✳ Nuts and seeds

✳ Eggs—the yolk contains iron and the white is high in protein and low in fat.

* Carbohydrates and whole grains (though a good source of protein, you'd need to eat a lot of grains to get enough protein).
* Rice—choose nonwhite if you can, or mix brown and white.
* Pasta—again, brown pasta is better.
* Potatoes—especially with the skins on
* Oats—oatmeal is a great way to start the day.
* Whole-grain cereals—avoid processed sweetened cereals.

Dairy

* Milk
* Yogurt—avoid highly sweetened ones; avoid low-fat or reduced-fat varieties, as they usually contain extra sugar or sweetener.
* Cheese

Fats

* Oils—olive, sunflower, flaxseed, grape seed, canola and nut. But these lose nutrients when cooked, so having them as a salad dressing is even better.
* Oily fish—tuna, mackerel, salmon, herring
* Avocados
* Nuts

Foods to have only occasionally:

These foods won't do much harm in small quantities, but try not to have them every day. Because it's important to be positive about foods rather than feeling guilty, I'm going to keep this simple by giving you only a very small list:

* Soda or sugary drinks
* Sweets and chocolate
* Chips
* Highly processed foods such as sausages and bacon

My philosophy is that if you eat enough of the healthy choices, you'll be full and won't crave sweet or processed things. And there's nothing wrong with cake or ice cream if you've had a good helping of nutritious food first.

See page 85 for some ideas about how you can actually incorporate those great choices into your day.

Are you a very fussy eater?

It's OK! It's very common to be cautious about new tastes, and to have lots of things you really don't like. Can you find eight things in the list of foods on pages 81 and 82 that you like, or at least don't dislike? If you can, there's no problem—just eat lots of them! Eat them first, so that you can eat as much of them as possible; then do your best to gradually grow your range of flavors. Set yourself a challenge of liking one extra thing by next month. Don't let food become a battleground. There are hundreds and hundreds of possibilities, and many more than I've suggested.

Do you need supplements?

If you eat a wide range of the foods I've suggested, you will get everything you need from your diet. Food supplements are not cheap and could be a waste of money. But some people may need them. If you fall into any of the categories below, get expert advice to make sure you're healthy and find out whether you need supplements:

✳ Vegans or other dietary choices that restrict a wide range of foods: it's not difficult to get all your nutrients from a vegan or almost any other diet, but you need to find sources of calcium, vitamin B_{12}, and iron. Get advice from appropriate national organizations for vegetarians, vegans, and the like.

✳ Girls who have started their periods: if you have heavy blood loss, you can lack iron. (See your doctor and don't take iron supplements without medical advice, as too much is not good for you. Iron is found in egg yolks and dark green vegetables, as well as in some red meat, but red meat is something we're told not to eat too often.)

✳ People who can't do much weight-bearing exercise: you may need extra calcium and vitamin D to help build bone mass. (Weight-bearing exercise means exercise that you do while supporting your own body weight on your legs or arms. People who have joint problems, weight problems, or disabilities that require a wheelchair fall into this category.)

✳ People who don't get much natural sunlight on their body (if they live in a very cold climate or don't go outside much) or people with dark skins (because melanin in their skin can block sunlight): sunlight helps the body produce vitamin D, so these people may need supplements.

✳ People with a specific medical condition that stops them from producing or processing certain nutrients: you will know if this applies to you.

SNACK IDEAS	SNACK IDEAS	MEAL IDEAS	MEAL IDEAS
dried berries	yogurt	lentil/veg soup + grilled cheese	eggs + whole-grain toast
mixed seeds/nuts	tuna fish or hummus + crackers	fish + salad	egg/tuna sandwich + salad
Brazil nuts	cheese + tomato sandwich	whole grain salad wrap + rice pudding	cheese/egg/chicken salad
homemade granola	avocado dip + carrots	oatmeal + boiled egg	chicken/tuna + pasta + salad
banana	apple + rice cake + cheese	baked eggplant + cheese on top	quiche + salad
shake with banana/berries	avocado toast	whole-wheat pancakes with fruit or savory stuffing	baked potato + cheese/beans + salad
dried fruit	bagel + cream cheese	salmon/mackerel/tuna + rice + peppers	salmon/tuna + rice + peas/salad
crackers + cheese	cottage cheese and breadsticks	stir-fry chicken, veg + noodles	salad with avocado + tomatoes
milk or hot chocolate	apple + peanut butter	chicken curry + rice + fruit salad	couscous + grilled chicken + salad

POSITIVELY YOU

A POSITIVE ATTITUDE

POSITIVELY HEALTHY

POSITIVELY BRAINY

POSITIVE ABOUT PEOPLE

A POSITIVE MOOD

POSITIVE BOOST

Take a fuel-boosting snack to school. Fill a container with nuts (if your school allows them), seeds, dried or fresh fruit, homemade granola, or whole-wheat crackers with cheese—though you'll need to eat this during the morning. If you can't manage breakfast before leaving home, you can eat this snack when you get to school.

And if you're hungry now, EAT!

Resources

EATING WELL

Healthy weight and BMI

Teens Health, part of the Kids Health website, has two places to calculate your BMI and find healthy advice:

http://kidshealth.org/en/teens/bmi.html

https://nccd.cdc.gov/dnpabmi/calculator.aspx

Healthy eating for teens

From nutrition.gov: *https://www.nutrition.gov/subject/life-stages /teens/tweens-and-teens*

From Kids Health: *http://kidshealth.org/en/teens/food-fitness/*

This one also has a Spanish version: *https://www.healthychildren .org/English/ages-stages/teen/nutrition/Pages/A-Teenagers -Nutritional-Needs.aspx*

Vegetarian and vegan health

Check out VegKitchen: *http://www.vegkitchen.com/nutrition /vegetarian-vegan-nutrition-teens*

From the Vegetarian Resource Group: *http://www.vrg.org/nutrition /teennutrition.htm*

Stay hydrated

You're often told to drink plenty of water, to prevent you from becoming "dehydrated"—literally "lacking water." It's fairly easy to do if you like drinking plain water, because that's certainly good for you. But you still need to think about how *much* water you need.

Also, what about other drinks? All liquids are basically water, but some liquids are less good at keeping you hydrated than others.

You'll find the facts about keeping hydrated, and helpful suggestions about what to drink, right here. So, read on!

POSITIVELY YOU

A POSITIVE ATTITUDE

POSITIVELY HEALTHY

POSITIVELY BRAINY

POSITIVE ABOUT PEOPLE

A POSITIVE MOOD

How much water?

It depends on how quickly you're losing water (through sweating, breathing, and peeing), and that depends on how hot you are, or how active. You get thirstier when it's hotter or when you're doing exercise. Feeling thirsty is the obvious sign that you need to drink more.

The other thing that makes it complicated is that other drinks and food *include* water. And it can be really hard to work out how much!

I'll give you two guidelines to help you decide whether you're drinking enough:

First—if you feel thirsty, you should definitely drink something. And you shouldn't wait to become very thirsty—ideally, aim to drink enough to *avoid* feeling thirsty. Keep some water with you when you can, and drink more in hot weather or when you're doing physical exercise.

Second—health organizations suggest we aim for at least six glasses of liquid a day in cool weather and eight glasses in warm weather or during activity. These figures are based on UK (six glasses) and US (eight glasses) government guidelines. You'll read arguments about which is right, or even whether either of them is right, but it is at least good to know what the "official" guidelines are.

You'll hear people say it's a myth that drinking water is good for us—it's not a myth! Drinking water is essential. What is *not* certain is whether drinking eight glasses is better than drinking six (or any other number you can come up with). Remember all the time that these figures *include* water in food and other drinks. I do think it's best not to obsess, though: just aim to drink enough so that you don't get to the thirsty stage.

What makes it more complicated is that we need to think about which drinks are "better" than others at giving us the right amount of water. Let's look at that now.

What drinks count?

All drinks are made mostly of water—that's why they're liquid. In fact, most foods contain a lot of water. For example, an apple is about 85 percent water. So, if you ate enough apples, in theory you'd have enough water. But getting all your water from apples would mean you'd eat more apples than was good for you! You'd probably get a stomachache, and if you did it regularly, you wouldn't consume enough other nutrients.

It does matter where we get our water, though. The simplest way is to drink plain water. Some other drinks are fine, but others have a few disadvantages, and we need to be aware of those. Then we can choose whether to drink them freely or drink them less often. So, let's look at the facts about various drinks.

Milk—a really healthy drink for most people; it certainly contributes well to water intake, but also has other nutrients. Whether you choose whole, 2 percent, or skim will depend on whether you are underweight or overweight, but 2 percent is appropriate for most people. There are also alternatives to dairy milk—such as almond, coconut, or soy milk—but these are often expensive. Experts disagree as to whether soy is good or bad, particularly in large quantities, and I suggest you talk to a dietician if you are planning to drink it or eat soybean products.

Fruit or herbal teas and other caffeine-free teas—these are fine as an alternative to some of your water intake.

Fruit juice—whether from concentrate or freshly squeezed fruits, fruit juices all contain acid (which is bad for teeth) and sugar. Even pure fruit juice with no added sugar still contains the natural sugar of the fruit. Also, sugar requires extra water to digest it. So, for many reasons, you shouldn't drink *too much* fruit juice, though a glass a day isn't a problem if you brush your teeth afterward. Ideally, drink juice with a meal rather than on its own. Fruit juice also has vitamins and a small amount of fiber if you drink it with pulp. All this also applies to smoothies.

Juice from concentrate or cordials—choose varieties that have no added sugar or artificial colors. The artificial sweeteners that replace the sugar in these drinks also cause health problems, and we are advised not to consume too much. So, whether you have sugar-free or sugary varieties, don't drink these juices too often and, when you do, dilute them with as much water as possible. You can get used to drinking juice very diluted, and eventually you might find you just prefer water. Water with a slice of lemon, lime, or orange is wonderful.

Soda/carbonated drinks—only for occasional treats, as there are some important problems: many contain a lot of sugar; the "diet" varieties contain large quantities of artificial sweeteners; they are not good for our teeth; and they often contain caffeine.

Caffeine—found in coffee, most teas, and some sodas and energy drinks. One problem with caffeine is that it is a "diuretic," which means that it takes water from your body by making you pee more. Therefore, you need to drink more liquid to replace what the caffeine removed. Experts say that if you drink a cup of any caffeinated liquid, you should only count

it as half a cup of water. Caffeine raises your heart rate and wakes you up, too, so avoid it completely during the evening.

Alcohol—I know you're not drinking alcohol, but I want to mention it anyway, so you know for the future. It's a diuretic, as well as having other serious health disadvantages. Alcohol doesn't count at all toward water intake.

What happens if we don't drink enough water?

Every part of your body needs water and you're losing it all the time—when you go to the bathroom, when you sweat, and every time you breathe. But the first things you'd probably notice would be headaches, feeling dizzy, and losing some concentration. You'll find it harder to do your best work. The brain has more water content than other parts of the body do, and that may be why it needs water to keep functioning well. Take a few swigs of water and you'll feel better almost immediately! Your headache may take a little longer to go away, but keeping your fluid levels up will help you focus and feel better.

Can we drink too much water?

Yes. Blood needs a complicated balance of salts, minerals, and chemicals. If you drink *too* much water, you dilute that balance and get sick. But you really need to drink a lot before you have a problem, so it's not likely. Just don't force yourself to drink.

If you're drinking a lot but still feeling thirsty, even when you're not exercising or feeling hot, see a doctor, just in case you have a problem, such as diabetes.

A word about salt

Salt makes us thirsty. How it does this is interesting: salt removes water from the blood, making our blood thicker and less watery; because this isn't healthy, the body deals with it by making us feel thirsty so we drink more.

Salt can be pretty unhealthy (though we do need some of it), and if we eat lots of salty things, we can get so used to it that we need more. But reducing our salt intake can be difficult because so many foods are high in salt: chips and most savory snacks, most processed food, most bread, most takeout, and many canned goods such as baked beans. It's often hidden in foods that don't even taste particularly salty.

Being careful about salt is even more important for adults—tell your parents! People with high blood pressure should be extra careful. But for most people the best thing is not to eliminate

POSITIVELY YOU

A POSITIVE ATTITUDE

POSITIVELY HEALTHY

POSITIVELY BRAINY

POSITIVE ABOUT PEOPLE

A POSITIVE MOOD

salt completely but not to add it to things and to go easy on foods that already taste salty. Drink extra water if you do eat something salty.

POSITIVE BOOST

Most people prefer iced water to warm. Make some flavored ice cubes by adding a small piece of any of the following to an ice cube tray before filling it with water: lemon, lime, or orange slice; mint or lemon balm leaf; fruit. It's fun and simple to do, and the act of making these gives you the chance to be creative and take a few moments out of your busy life.

Resources

DRINKING ENOUGH

This is a good site from Australia: *www.healthykids.nsw.gov.au/kids -teens/stats-and-facts-teens/teens-nutrition/drinks-for-hydration.aspx*

An interesting article showing that we need to keep hydrated, but don't need to count eight glasses of water to do it: *www.care2.com /greenliving/8-common-myths-about-dehydration.html*

The power of oxygen

O_2 Oxygen is in the air we breathe, of course. Without it, we quickly die. We don't have to think about breathing, but there are a couple of situations where you might not be getting the ideal amount of oxygen. If you are aware of this, it's very easy to deal with it. The strategies I'll give you will make an instant difference in how you feel and how your brain and body work.

It's useful to think about what is in the air we breathe. We tend to say that we breathe in oxygen and breathe out carbon dioxide. But the truth is more complicated. The air we breathe in is mostly nitrogen (about 78 percent), while oxygen makes up about 20 percent. There are also other gases, including a small amount of carbon dioxide. The figures change depending on how high above sea level we are and other factors. On a mountain, there will be much less oxygen. So, the air we breathe in does not always contain the same amount of oxygen.

Assuming you're not about to climb a mountain, let's look at two situations where you might have less oxygen than is ideal. (By the way, people who live on mountains adapt to less oxygen, and they can manage well!)

POSITIVELY YOU
A POSITIVE ATTITUDE
POSITIVELY HEALTHY
POSITIVELY BRAINY
POSITIVE ABOUT PEOPLE
A POSITIVE MOOD

First, think about times when you've been sitting in the same room for a while. Maybe it's your bedroom at home and the door and window are shut, or maybe it's a classroom with lots of people breathing the same air. Since you breathe in oxygen and breathe out carbon dioxide, after a while there's not as much oxygen in the room as there was. It feels stuffy. There's more carbon dioxide and less oxygen.

The simple strategy is to get up, go out of the room, and take a very short walk or do something energizing like going up stairs. Obviously, you might not be able to do this in the middle of class! But even asking to open the window will help. Many teachers understand this and find that getting students to stand up and walk around or do some running in place makes them able to work better afterward.

Moving around makes your heartbeat and breathing faster, so more oxygen goes through your lungs. From there, the oxygen is carried in your blood, all around your body, including to your brain.

Basically, the first tip is: if you've been sitting down for a while, get up, move around, and ideally go outside. This also applies if you've been sitting down for a while playing computer games or video games, or using your smartphone or other device. This can become really unhealthy for body and brain, so one very important positively healthy tip is to avoid sitting down for longer than an hour at a time.

Second, when you are stressed or nervous, your breathing will probably become too shallow. Try this activity to test your breathing right now:

Keep breathing just as you were. Place one hand high on your chest, with your thumb at the base of your throat, and the other hand below your rib cage, on your stomach. Just breathe normally a few times. Which hand moves more? If it's the hand near your throat, your breathing is too shallow—you may be anxious and stressed. You won't be getting enough oxygen into your body, and you may feel dizzy or your concentration

POSITIVE BOOST

If you've been sitting for a while, get up now. Stretch as tall as you can, breathing deeply and slowly. As you breathe in, raise your arms high into the air. As you breathe out, bring them slowly down while stretching them to the side in a big arc. Do this a few times. Then go for a two-minute walk around the house. Do this whenever you've been working for more than forty-five minutes at home.

Or, if you can't go outside, lie on your back. Raise your knees toward your chest and roll your hips upward so they are off the ground; place your hands beneath your hips; and do some upside-down cycling with your legs.

may start to fail. Relaxed breathing is sometimes called "belly breathing" because it's the "belly" that moves more. That sort of breathing tends to be slower and deeper.

So, deep breathing will help you get more oxygen into your bloodstream. Don't do it too much, too deeply, or for too long, though, or you might feel faint or even actually faint, as the oxygen and carbon dioxide levels in your blood will become imbalanced.

Sleeping with a window open is a good idea. Of course, it isn't always possible, but try it if you can. There are special locks that only allow a window to be opened a tiny bit for safety.

Just getting outside to inhale fresher air can also make you feel much better instantly. It clears your head, helps you focus, improves mood, and generally affects your physical and mental health in positive ways.

POSITIVELY YOU

A POSITIVE ATTITUDE

POSITIVELY HEALTHY

POSITIVELY BRAINY

POSITIVE ABOUT PEOPLE

A POSITIVE MOOD

Sunlight on your skin

Sunlight helps the body produce vitamin D, which is essential for strong bones. That's because the calcium we ingest builds strong bones, but without vitamin D the calcium isn't properly absorbed.

People who don't have enough vitamin D can have weaker bones and might develop a condition called rickets, where bones become softer and may bend outward—"bowed legs." Rickets was common among people with poor diets before we knew about vitamin D, and it's still quite common in colder countries and poorer communities. Vitamin D may also protect against serious illnesses later. Because of all this, it's often added to "fortified" cereals. To see whether it's in the cereal you eat, look at the list of nutrients on the box. But those cereals often also contain a lot of sugar, so we shouldn't consume too much of them.

We get some vitamin D from food, but it's hard to get enough that way because it's found only in a small number of foods (oily fish, some red meat, and eggs), so we really need sunlight. Besides, it feels great to have the sun on our skin. It usually raises people's spirits!

One problem, however, is that the sun is dangerous, causing long-term damage to skin and extra risk of skin cancer later. So, how can you get the right amount safely?

First, spend enough time outside. (Looking through a window doesn't help, because the "UVB" rays don't go through glass.) In a cold climate, this can be difficult, especially in winter months. But try to go outside every day if you can.

Second, expose more than just your face, which is hard if you need to bundle up in a coat and gloves. When you can, roll your sleeves up and your socks down and get that sunlight on your skin.

Third, go outside even when it's not sunny. If you're outside on a moderately dull day, there's still some light coming through the clouds. When the sun is higher (between 11 AM and 3 PM), you have a better chance of getting enough sunlight.

Fourth, everyone's needs are different. If you have darker skin—Asian or African coloring, for example—you need to spend longer in the sun to make the same amount of vitamin D, but even people with very dark skin can burn, so be careful.

How to make sure you don't burn

Different skin types make a huge difference in how much sun is safe. Younger skin tends to be more delicate, too. Here are some things that mean you have to be more careful than other people in the sun, as you are at greater risk of sunburn and skin cancer later:

* Skin that tends to go pink in the sun easily

* Lots of moles or freckles

* Fair or light coloring—blond hair, blue eyes, and pale skin

* A history of skin cancer in your family

People with darker skin can still burn and risk all the same problems; it's just that they can tolerate the sun for longer periods of time.

And sunburn risk doesn't occur only when the weather is obviously hot and sunny. It depends on some other things, too:

✳ Time of year—in the US and northern Europe, the sun is closest to you between April and September; near the equator, it's close to you all year round; in the southern parts of South America or southern Australia, it is closest between November and March.

✳ Altitude—if you're on mountains, you're closer to the sun.

✳ Type of cloud cover—whether it is thick or thin

✳ Logistics—if you are on sand, snow, or water, some of the sun's rays are reflected back at you, giving you greater exposure.

People often get sunburned when they are not sunbathing. They might be doing an activity, not feeling particularly hot, and just not thinking about the sun. Often, a breeze makes us feel nice and cool, but the sun can be doing damage anyway.

Another useful thing is to look out for the "UV index" for the day. You'll find this on the Internet, on weather apps, and on weather reports during the summer months wherever you are in the world.

Don't take risks with the sun: use a high-SPF sunscreen, and don't expose your skin to the sun for too long. You can still burn through light cloud cover, and a cool breeze can prevent you from noticing how hot it is. Go outside for short periods at a time and don't wait to feel tingling or redness before you cover up or go inside.

A suntan is a sign of damage. So, what we're aiming for is to get enough sunlight without having any visible effects. Little and often is the key.

Do you need to take vitamin D supplements?

During summer months, most of you won't need supplements, unless you are unable to go outdoors much or you cover your skin for cultural or other reasons.

During the winter, especially if you spend most of your time indoors, or if there's any reason why you don't get much sunlight, taking a supplement could be a good idea.

Studies over the last ten years suggest that vitamin D deficiency is a growing problem in the US, and that deficiency among young people is increasing in various other countries.

Only an expert can confirm whether this is an issue for you: talk it over with a school nurse, doctor, or dietician. It will depend on your diet, skin type, where you live, and the state of your health. There will be no harm in taking the recommended amount as a supplement, but never take more than that unless advised by an expert. And remember that it's always best to try to get the right amount of nutrients naturally, not from supplements. Taking too much of certain vitamins can be dangerous.

Resources

HEALTHY USE OF THE SUN

How to know whether your skin type is more likely to burn and the facts you need: www.senseaboutscienceusa.org/sun-risk-skin-cancer-different-groups/

Be active

It's obvious that physical activity is good for our bodies, but did you know that it's *very* good for our brains? It's good for our whole mental and physical well-being.

Lots of experts say exercise is the most important part of being healthy, helping us avoid many serious illnesses, feel better about ourselves, and generally have a much more positive outlook.

I'll let you know the benefits, and then I'll tell you how you can find something that suits you, even if you don't think you want to exercise or don't think you can. There is something for everyone, no matter what your ability!

Having said that, before changing your level of exercise significantly, you should get medical advice, in case there's a reason why you should avoid certain activities.

What good does exercise do?

Different exercise has different benefits. To have an all-around effect, you need a combination of aerobic exercise that gets you out of breath (such as brisk walking, dancing, or jogging) and muscle-building or "resistance" exercise that involves pushing and pulling (such as push-ups, sit-ups, or using small weights). There are also stretching exercises that protect muscles and make you more flexible.

Exercise has these benefits if you do a variety of different types:

✱ Strengthens your heart. The heart is a muscle, and it gets stronger when it has to work a bit harder some of the time. You shouldn't overdo it, but for most people it's good to raise the heart rate about three times a week.

✱ Increases the amount of oxygen your body can use, by improving how much your lungs can take in.

✱ Protects your joints by building muscles around them. (Over-exercise can damage joints, though, so if you do something a lot, it's important to get advice from a sports expert, such as your PE teacher or someone working at the local gym or swimming pool.)

✱ Builds bone strength, so you're less likely to break bones when you're older. For this you need "weight-bearing" exercise. For example, jogging helps strengthen bones in the legs, and using weights builds bones in the arms or legs. (Again, doing too much can have the opposite effect: for example, people who jog too much on hard surfaces can get fractures in their shinbones.)

✱ Improves mood. There's tons of evidence about this now, and many mental health experts encourage anyone who suffers from mental illness to try to exercise. Any time you're feeling down, a little exercise, even going for a quick walk, is likely to have an immediate positive effect.

∗ Improves how your brain works, including concentration and focus, as well as memory and organization skills.

∗ Helps you process what you've just learned. A number of studies have looked at the effects of learning something and then doing physical exercise. Results suggest that physical exercise helps your brain process what you've learned, so that you recall it better later.

∗ Helps your brain produce new neurons (those nerve cells that carry messages around your brain and down your spinal cord). Years ago, people thought we didn't make new neurons, but now it seems we do, and one of the things that can trigger this is physical exercise. Scientists believe this because of studies showing that mice grow neurons when they spend a lot of time running around their wheel.

∗ Helps you sleep. It may be partly because exercise improves our mood, and that can help you sleep, but there's also evidence that doing exercise earlier in the day tends to give us better sleep. Don't do energetic exercises in the evening, though: do them earlier in the day and just do gentle stretches or yoga to relax before bed.

What if you don't like exercise or can't do it?

Some people love being active, but others say they don't. And there are lots of obstacles that might make it difficult to get a healthy level of exercise.

One problem is that when we think about exercise, we think about getting hot and sweaty; being out of breath; feeling competitive, aggressive, or self-conscious; or even getting hurt. But "being active" does not have to involve any of those things! I believe there is a physical activity for everyone, something out there that you can enjoy even if you *think* you can't. So, people who say they don't enjoy it are perhaps thinking about the wrong kinds of exercise.

Being active can mean just going for a walk, bowling, dancing, doing some stretches in your room, or walking up and down the stairs. It can be social or it can be solitary. You don't have to join a team or a class if you don't want to. You just have to not sit down too much.

Sitting too much is unhealthy. If you investigate the phrase "sedentary lifestyle," you'll find lots of research about the health problems associated with sitting for too long. ("Sedentary" literally means "sitting.")

I'm a writer, so I have to sit for long periods of time. Or do I? Actually, no. I write standing up. To be accurate, I write while walking on an office treadmill! Obviously, this isn't something you can do at school or even at home, I assume, but it illustrates that there are ways to get exercise even if you have to "sit" a lot.

EXERCISING WITH A DISABILITY

What about people who *have* to sit: people in wheelchairs, for a start? What happens if you are disabled, so it's difficult or impossible for you to get up and be active? How are you supposed to react to being told to get more exercise?

Well, I'm talking about doing what you can. Disabilities vary, but there is always something you can do to raise your heart rate. Not everyone can achieve the amazing results of the Paralympians, just as not every able-bodied person can reach elite levels, either—especially me! But what disabled athletes show is that there are many ways of using your body actively, many ways of being *able*, even if you are *dis*abled in some way. Exercising with your arms raises your heart rate, for example. Any physical activity that makes your heart go faster has all the same benefits as

POSITIVELY YOU

A POSITIVE ATTITUDE

POSITIVELY HEALTHY

POSITIVELY BRAINY

POSITIVE ABOUT PEOPLE

A POSITIVE MOOD

those for able-bodied people. And whichever parts of your body work best are the ones you can use for exercising. Your doctor or occupational therapist will be happy to help you find something you can do, and most local communities offer suitable activities for everybody.

If you have any disability, follow these guidelines as much as possible and then get extra help from doctors and experts for your specific condition.

How much exercise should you do?

Of course, if you have an illness or disability, check with your doctor first in case different guidelines apply. Otherwise, it's recommended that teens should be active for at least an hour every day. But this does not mean you have to do *organized sports* for an hour every day! It just means being as active as possible, rather than sitting still.

Experts also recommend a mixture of three sorts of activity:

✱ Activity that raises the heart rate. This can be "moderate," which means that you can talk *as you exercise,* but not sing a song. Examples might include fast walking or cycling. Or the activity can be "vigorous," which means you'd be unable to talk while doing it. Examples might be running, dancing, or soccer.

✱ Activity that strengthens bones. This is any activity that uses your legs or arms in a way that creates an "impact" or pressure. So, consider anything involving running or jumping (for the legs) or weight training, gymnastics, or tennis (for arms and legs).

✱ Activity that strengthens muscles. Most exercise will strengthen some muscles, but ideally you want to strengthen lots of muscles, so you'll need to think of some different activities. Muscles are especially strengthened when we do things that involve lifting our own weight (such as push-ups or pull-ups) or have a resistance against something (such as weights, a ball/racket).

104

Some simple and fun examples

Here are some exercises you might think about trying. Not all of them will be suitable for you, so just choose the ones you think might work. Then use your imagination to think of more!

★ With a friend, go to the local park and walk around it several times. Do one minute of fast walking followed by two or three minutes of slow walking.

★ Walk on your own while listening to music. Again, do a minute of fast walking followed by two or three minutes of gentle walking.

★ In your room, dance to your favorite music (with headphones if you want to!). You can even just dance with your arms.

★ Don't use an elevator or escalator—use the stairs.

★ Go swimming.

★ Go online and find workouts that suit you. You'll find some that are free and cater to all ages and abilities.

★ At your local sports center or at school, join a yoga class or any other class that interests you. Go with a friend if you want to.

★ Walk up and down the stairs in your house several times. Count how many you manage before giving up. See if you can do more tomorrow.

★ Climb a tree. (Be careful, but if you have somewhere you can safely climb, this is a great exercise. It's good for balance, core stability, and strength. Some adults are going to criticize me for suggesting tree-climbing, because it's usually unsupervised and there's a risk of injury. I'm going to trust you to do it carefully with friends. Don't be too ambitious and don't go too high. Be positively responsible for your own safety.)

★ Fly a kite.

★ When walking to the store or to school or the bus stop, walk faster!

★ Check out YouTube for some exercise videos appropriate to your age and level of fitness.

★ Buy an exercise band—a rubber strip that allows you to do a lot of strength exercises in your own time and in privacy.

★ Go to your local library and see what classes or activities are advertised.

★ Learn how to do a few exercises correctly, so you can do them on your own. Your PE teacher would be happy to show you!

★ Plan ahead. Make a chart to remind yourself what to do each day and record what you did.

★ Remember to include all the activity you have to do at school. And even if you don't like it, be as active as possible, because it all counts toward your health.

If you look at **Have a hobby** on page 135, you'll see a list of other physical activities that young people can do to give you some more ideas.

An important warning: be careful not to exercise too much. If you're an athlete or training for a competition, you will be doing a lot of exercise, of course, but you'll have a coach whose job it is to make sure that you also eat and drink properly and are not doing anything that might cause problems in the future. If you exercise excessively, without expert supervision, you could cause long-term health issues for yourself.

When you exercise, have something healthy to eat and drink afterward to replace the energy your body has used up.

Exercise is fantastic for a positive lifestyle, but it's possible to do too much. Work out enough to keep you healthy, but not so much that you cause yourself harm, lower your energy levels, or develop an unhealthy relationship with exercise. It should be something to enjoy and to make you feel great, rather than something that becomes a compulsion.

Let exercise be part of being positively teen.

Resources

HEALTHY EXERCISE

Why be active?

WebMD: *https://teens.webmd.com/benefits-of-exercise#1*

Kids Health: *http://kidshealth.org/en/teens/exercise-wise.html*

The Brainflux website details many benefits of exercise and offers links to research for each, including improving willpower, concentration, memory, and sleep: *http://thebrainflux.com/brain-benefits-of -exercise/*

How much activity?

The US official guidelines for young people are one hour a day: *https:// health.gov/paguidelines/guidelines/chapter3.aspx*

World Health Organization guidelines: *http://www.who.int /dietphysicalactivity/factsheet_young_people/en/*

Research

Mood: *www.ncbi.nlm.nih.gov/pmc/articles/PMC1424736/pdf /pubhealthrep00100-0085.pdf*

Improving higher brain functions, including planning: *www.ncbi.nlm .nih.gov/pubmed/2322944*

Improving concentration: *www.pnas.org/content/101/9/3316.abstract*

Short-term memory: *https://www.ncbi.nlm.nih.gov/pubmed/25304335*

Long-term memory: *www.ncbi.nlm.nih.gov/pmc/articles/PMC2897704/*

An article in the *Guardian* newspaper, on research suggesting that different activities have different effects on your brain: *www .theguardian.com/education/2016/jun/18/how-physical-exercise -makes-your-brain-work-better*

Growing neurons: *www.ncbi.nlm.nih.gov/pmc/articles/PMC1360197/*

A TED talk on this from neuroscientist Sandrine Thuret: *www.ted.com /talks/sandrine_thuret_you_can_grow_new_brain_cells_here_s_how /transcript?language=en*

Sleeping better

The Sleep Foundation: *sleepfoundation.org/sleep-news/study -physical-activity-impacts-overall-quality-sleep*

Too much sitting is unhealthy

Teens: *physicalactivityteens.weebly.com/consequences-of -physical-inactivity-in-teenagers.html*

Activity for young people with disabilities

PBS: *https://www.pbs.org/newshour/show/empowering-students -disabilities-find-exercise-love*

Centers for Disease Control and Prevention: *https://www.cdc.gov /features/physical-activity-disabilities/index.html*

Ideas for yoga-type exercises for short breaks

Kids Health: *kidshealth.org/en/teens/yoga-break.html?WT .ac=ctg#catstudysmart*

Sleep well

Sleep is a weird thing if you think about it. There's such a big and mysterious difference between being conscious, in control, and thinking coherently, and being unconscious, out of control, and having weird dreams instead of rational thoughts. What goes on in our brain and body while we sleep? What is sleep *for*? How important is it, and what happens if we don't get enough? I'll answer those questions first and then help you learn how to fall asleep more quickly and get better sleep.

People used to think sleep was simply for rest and to build up energy. It certainly does that. But we know now there's much more to it.

Thousands of years ago, sleep would have been dangerous: while you were asleep, a predator or enemy could attack you. This applies to all living creatures, and each species has evolved its own way to sleep safely. For example, dolphins and whales sleep with one half of their brain asleep at a time. They are "conscious breathers" and can only breathe when they remember to, whereas we breathe even when we're unconscious. Some animals go to sleep for the winter, to avoid having to eat when there's not much food. Many animals—such as cats—have lots of short naps and are able to snap awake quickly.

The sleep cycle

Humans usually have one long sleep during the hours of darkness, but we aren't in deep sleep all that time. We have five or six cycles of sleep, each one about an hour and a half long. During each cycle, we go through five stages of sleep. And each one is important in different ways.

✳ **Stage one** is a short period of light sleep. If something wakes you during this time, you won't feel groggy, and you'll think you've barely been asleep at all.

Lots of creative ideas happen during this stage. Some artists and scientists try to wake themselves up at this point so that they can access their creativity. Scientist Albert Einstein and artist Salvador Dalí both did this. Dalí used to take a nap holding a metal spoon in his hand, which was dangling over a metal tray. As he relaxed into sleep, the spoon would drop, waking him up with the clatter, and he would write down whatever thoughts were in his head at the time.

✳ **Stage two** is also a fairly light sleep. It lasts about twenty minutes during the early parts of the night, but less later on. This is a restful stage for your brain, and there is little activity in the thinking, learning, and problem-solving areas. Scientists believe this is the stage that is most important for strengthening networks for physical skills such as those used for music, gymnastics, and other sports, or operating devices and tools—things that you have to learn "how to do."

✳ **Stages three** and **four** are much deeper, with your body relaxed and brain activity very slow. If someone tries to wake you, they will find it difficult, and if something or someone does force you awake, you'll feel groggy and disoriented. These deep-sleep stages are important for physical and mental well-being. It's during this time that your body produces growth hormones. This obviously helps you grow at the right speed, but it's also important for repairing damage to cells. During these stages, your brain repeats things you were focusing on during the day. Suppose you were practicing a musical instrument and struggling to play the piece well, or you were playing basketball and becoming frustrated at making mistakes, or trying to understand some math problem or learn some history: your brain will practice those actions and thought processes, and even clear away some of the faulty brain networks. The sleeping brain does a lot of clearing away of dead cells and broken connections during this stage. The spaces between your neurons expand to let more fluid through—a bit like washing the kitchen floor!

You are not dreaming during any of these stages. You may have random thoughts, images, or ideas, but these are not the sort of things we call dreams, where whole stories take place.

✱ **Stage five** is the dreaming stage. It's often called REM sleep. REM stands for "rapid eye movement" because that's what happens when you're in it! If you ever watch someone in REM sleep, you'll see their eyelids twitch. Behind the eyelids their eyes are moving fast.

During this stage, your brain is *very* active, almost as if you're awake, but your body is paralyzed, so you don't usually act out your dreams. (Unless you sleepwalk, which is a sleep disorder that is more common in children than adults. It's not usually a problem, but it can be worrying and exhausting. So, if you are doing this, you should get advice from a doctor. One of the main causes is sleep deprivation, so going to bed earlier could help.)

Scientists are beginning to unlock the mysteries of dreaming, but they still don't know everything. They believe that REM sleep is important to mental health, allowing us to process difficult or traumatic events. It also seems to help us build strong memories, and can sometimes enable us to work out solutions to problems.

112

How much sleep do you need?

Everyone is a bit different, and some differences depend on age. On average, a healthy adult needs about eight hours, and a healthy teenager a little over nine. We seem to be able to *get by* on less than that, but those numbers are good to aim for.

You might be wondering if it's OK to get our sleep in small chunks rather than one long period of time? Well, it's better to do that than not get enough, but it's best to get it all at once. Remember I said that we usually have five or six sleep cycles of roughly one and a half hours each? The thing is that although the cycles are roughly the same length, the earlier ones have more light sleep and less deep sleep, whereas the later ones have more deep sleep. So, if you have too little sleep overall, you'll miss some deep sleep. People who work night shifts and have irregular or short sleep sessions usually find it has a negative effect on mood and performance.

But we all have times when we can't get enough sleep. When that happens, we shouldn't worry about it. We just need to do our best to get back to a healthy level.

What about daytime naps—do they count?

Yes, they can (if you're lucky enough to get the chance!). They can be a really good idea. But try not to sleep for longer than twenty minutes or you'll wake feeling groggy.

What happens when we don't get enough?

At first, nothing. Obviously, you might feel a bit tired the next day. But you definitely shouldn't be stressed about one really bad night's sleep, especially before an exam or something else you're worried about. The chemical adrenaline, from nerves and excitement, will give you the energy you need.

But if you regularly don't get enough sleep, you're likely to notice the following: feeling sick; not being able to concentrate; making mistakes; not doing your best work at school; being in a bad mood; and finding it harder to control your response to anger or other emotions. These things can lead to problems with friendships and affect your schoolwork. They're also likely to affect how well your brain learns.

Just ask yourself this: do you think your schoolwork is as good as it could be? If you think it could be better, maybe getting more sleep would help.

How can you get a good night's sleep?

This is the most important question of all, and I have some strategies based on strong science! And tell this to the adults in your life, because all of this applies to them, too. During the hour or two before you want to feel sleepy, think about the following principles:

* Make your brain think it's later at night than it is by removing daylight from your room. You may need thick curtains or blackout blinds. Close them at least an hour and a half before you want to sleep.

* Create a routine to trick your brain into thinking it's bedtime. You can choose a few things to do in the same order each evening before getting into bed and turning the light off. The brain loves a routine and will quickly learn to recognize this as your pre-bed routine. (Choose anything from the list of Sleep Positives on page 115.)

* Calm your brain and body down. This involves only doing things from the Sleep Positives list, and never doing things from the Sleep Negatives list, during the hour and a half before bedtime.

Sleep Positives

* Switch off all devices such as the TV, computer, phone, and tablet.

* Switch off bright lights and close curtains or blinds.

* Have a small snack if you're hungry—something dairy- or carbohydrate-based: a sandwich, for example, or a glass of milk and a banana.

* Put your work away and get things ready for the morning.

* Get undressed and ready for bed.

* Take a bath or shower.

* Listen to slow, soft music.

* Do gentle stretching or yoga.

* Read a book or listen to a podcast.

Sleep Negatives

* Bright lights

* All screen-based devices

* Loud noise

* Excitement, anger, stress

* Fast exercise

* Caffeinated drinks—coffee, ordinary tea, and soda, for example

* Too much food

★ Create your own sleep routine

Your routine will work so much better if you have chosen it yourself. Here's what to do:

Decide what time you plan to get into bed.

Plan to begin the first item of your routine between sixty and ninety minutes before this.

★ The routine should always include removing daylight from your room. This means both through the window (with thick curtains or blackout blinds) and from screens. So, your first item should ideally be to finish all screen-based things so you can turn them off.

★ Besides "remove daylight" and "turn off screens," choose approximately five items from the list of Sleep Positives. You can also add your own things if you are sure they are good for pre-sleep—ask an adult if you're not sure.

★ "Get into bed" should obviously be in there! Once in bed, you can read a book or do anything gently relaxing. (No online or mobile-connected activity, of course!)

Put everything on a list, in the order you think is best.

Start your routine today if it's not too late. Always do the things in the same order. You should notice yourself sleeping more easily after a week or so. If you don't, keep going. It's still a very healthy way to prepare for sleep.

How to get to sleep when it feels impossible

This is something almost everyone experiences. Often it's when a thought goes around and around in your mind. Sometimes it's when you're really excited and can't calm down. And other times it's when you are overstimulated by lights, noise, screens, or unusual things that happened during the day.

Here's the best advice:

✳ Stop thinking about sleep. Stop even trying to sleep. It doesn't matter right now.

✳ If the cause is anxiety, write what's worrying you on a piece of paper. Then fold the paper several times and put it by the door. Tell yourself there's nothing more you can do about it and you'll sort it out tomorrow if possible. If that isn't possible, thinking about it now won't help.

✳ Fix anything that's making you uncomfortable: needing to go to the bathroom, being too cold or hot, adjusting wrinkly sheets.

✳ Slow your breathing a little. Focus on it. Count slow breaths until you feel calmer—do it for several minutes, if you like.

✳ Now, *visualize* your perfect place. It can be somewhere you've been or somewhere in your imagination. Build up the detail. Where are you: garden, beach, bed, vacation, alone or with friends? What can you see: colors, trees, beach, sea, clouds, birds? What can you smell: sunscreen, cake, ocean, scented candles? What can you hear: waves, cars, people, wind, nothing? How do you feel: warm, peaceful, relaxed, calm? Think of your fingers, toes, stomach, the skin on your face. If any bad thoughts come in, just let them go and focus back on what you want to think about.

Don't worry if this doesn't work quickly. It's good that you're resting and relaxed. Try not to think about sleep: just focus on whatever positive thoughts you like. If you can't fall asleep for a while, you can choose to either continue lying there, resting, and breathing slowly, or you can read a book or listen to very soft music. Don't be tempted to turn on your phone or other Internet-enabled device.

Sleep is a really important part of looking after yourself. It might feel like something you can't control, and to some extent that's true, at least sometimes. But there are things you *can* do that will help. You have the tools now. When you really can't sleep, don't stress about it.

POSITIVELY YOU

A POSITIVE ATTITUDE

POSITIVELY HEALTHY

POSITIVELY BRAINY

POSITIVE ABOUT PEOPLE

A POSITIVE MOOD

I have to say this one more time because it's the most important thing for a good night's sleep, for adults, too: switch off all digital devices well before bedtime. It will help, trust me!

Resources

SLEEP
Getting better sleep

From Kids Health: *kidshealth.org/en/teens/tips-sleep.html? WT.ac=p-ra*

From the Sleep Doctor: *https://www.thesleepdoctor.com/2017/03/30 /teens-need-sleep-think*

From the National Sleep Foundation: *https://sleepfoundation.org /sleep-topics/teens-and-sleep*

From the Cleveland Clinic: *https://my.clevelandclinic.org/health /articles/adolescent-sleep/tips*

Effects of sleep on memory/learning

From Harvard University: *healthysleep.med.harvard.edu/healthy /matters/benefits-of-sleep/learning-memory*

While you're asleep, toxins in your brain are cleared away!

From the National Institutes of Health: *https://www.nih.gov/news -events/nih-research-matters/how-sleep-clears-brain*

Sleepwalking

From the Sleep Foundation: *sleepfoundation.org/sleep-disorders -problems/abnormal-sleep-behaviors/sleepwalking/page/0/1*

Summing up

In this section, you've learned so many practical ways to look after your well-being and be healthy. You know how to make sure you're eating enough, and I've given you lots of options when it comes to choosing the right types of food to make you healthy.

You've learned about the importance of drinking enough water and getting sunlight on your skin, and you've found out how to breathe properly to help concentration and mood.

You've discovered the importance of getting exercise for the health of your body, and also your brain. You've found out how important sleep is to your well-being and how to get a good night's sleep.

There is so much you can do to maintain control and have a positive effect on your own life and health. Your body and brain will thank you!

Positively Brainy

Your brain is amazing! It's responsible for everything you can do and everything you feel and think. It's your control center, and it contains all your memories and everything you know, as well as the keys to your personality. But your brain is not fixed: it's changing all the time. Everything you do makes a difference to your brain, setting down a physical pathway that makes that thing easier the next time. Scientists don't yet know everything about the human brain, but we know much more than we did when your parents were children. And one thing we know is that there are things we can do to make our brains work better for us, so that we can have greater control over our lives and our success. That's what this section is about.

All the other things in this book—eating well, sleeping, exercising, being social, having a positive attitude—help, too. But this section focuses on particular things that directly affect how your brain works.

Are you ready to become positively brainy?

Practice makes perfect

People have probably been saying this for hundreds of years, but you might have noticed that it's not always true! It's often not possible to become "perfect." You could become perfect at spelling the word "immediately," but you couldn't necessarily be perfect at swimming or soccer or at math or at kindness or at knowing what to say to a friend who's upset. You could try to become perfect at gymnastics or singing, but I think even the world's best gymnasts and singers probably want to be even better than they are.

But practice *does* make us better at whatever we are trying to become better at. And this practice does something particular in our brains.

What I'm about to say is perhaps the most important thing to know about how the brain works. Knowing this will give you power and a positive attitude about anything you might want to become good at. Are you ready?

How the brain learns

I talked about this in a different way in the introduction to A POSITIVE ATTITUDE on page 46. There, I was talking about how the brain makes pathways for positive and negative thoughts, by repeating them. So, what I'm about to say about how the brain learns will feel familiar.

When we do something—move a finger, speak, remember the capital of Spain—electrical messages have to pass along the correct pathways between neurons. We are born with 85 to 100 billion neurons.

When we're born, most of these neurons aren't connected into pathways, so electrical signals can't travel, and newborn babies can't do much. Also, when we start to learn a new skill at any age, the neurons we need haven't formed strong pathways, which is why the first time we try something, it's usually difficult.

If we want to become good at something, we have to grow connections between the right neurons, so that strong pathways form and the electrical signals can travel easily. The connections are like branches (called dendrites, which is from the ancient Greek word for "tree") that reach out and *almost* touch the next neuron. The place where they almost touch is called a synapse, and the space is so tiny that the electrical signals can jump across.

Growing these connections is easy! Here's how we do it:

By watching someone else do it. When we watch someone, our own brain activates neurons called mirror neurons, which start imitating the person we are watching. Then, when we try to do it ourselves, it's a little easier because our brain has actually already started practicing, so pathways have begun to form.

By trying—even if we fail. Every time we try to do something, we physically build connections. The more we try, the more connections grow and the stronger they become. This is how practicing makes us better: we are physically building connections and pathways in our brain.

By sleeping! You learned about this on page 112. Sleep is crucial for learning. You may remember that during certain stages of sleep, your brain "practices" the things you were trying to do during the day. Your brain is practicing for you, while you're asleep. (I did say your brain was amazing!)

The point is, every time our brain repeats something, it creates a stronger pathway, making it easier to do next time. If you're finding something difficult, remember that each time you practice, you *are* getting better. Sometimes the improvement is too small to notice, but it all adds up. Remember the "growth mind-set"? We become good at things by trying and doing.

Practice might not make perfect, but it does make it better.

But what if you keep repeating a mistake? What if you don't know how to do something and need some help? Let's take a look at how to practice *well*.

Good practicing

SPACED LEARNING

If we want to learn something and remember it for a long time, it's best to do it in several separate sessions rather than try to learn it all at once. Back in 1885, Hermann Ebbinghaus discovered what he called the "forgetting curve," showing how we forget over time, and then he found ways to prevent this from happening. He discovered that if we repeat lessons with increasing amounts of time between each session, information goes into our long-term memory and is hard to forget. It's called spaced repetition, or spaced learning.

This works especially well for learning vocabulary or dates or facts.

★ Let's test the theory!

I'm going to give you two verses of a poem to remember. You can use whatever methods you like—writing or speaking or decorating with colors or whatever you want—but you should use the same method for each.

When you learn the first verse, do this: spend seven minutes learning it now; then spend seven minutes learning it tomorrow; then six minutes two days after that (twenty minutes spaced into three sessions).

When you learn the second verse, do this: spend twenty minutes learning it all in one sitting today. Do not look at it again (twenty minutes not spaced out at all).

Five days from now, see if you can recite the verses without looking. Which one did you find easier?

Verse 1

He thought he saw an Elephant
That practiced on a fife:
He looked again, and found it was
A letter from his wife.

"At length I realize," he said,
"The bitterness of life!"

Verse 2

He thought he saw a Buffalo
Upon the chimney-piece:
He looked again, and found it was
His Sister's Husband's Niece.

"Unless you leave this house," he said,
"I'll send for the police!"

(First two verses of "A Strange Wild Song" by Lewis Carroll)

TAKING BREAKS

There are two reasons why taking breaks is good and why they help you learn. First, you sometimes do need a rest. Studying is tiring! That's not surprising, because your brain uses energy.

Second, it seems that taking a break to do something different helps the information go into the right parts of the brain. So, if you're trying to learn or understand something, while you take a break your brain continues to process the information. That's why when you come back to it, you've learned it a bit better.

The best things to do during the breaks include:

* Physical exercise—even just a quick walk outside

* Social activity—face-to-face, not on-screen

* Sleep—not more than twenty minutes

Is it better to take a break after finishing a piece of work or before finishing? Research suggests that it is probably better to do it *before*! Unfinished tasks hang around in the memory— a bit like leaving a page open on your computer so you can come back to it quickly. It also seems that the best time to interrupt your task with a break is when you're concentrating on it most! When you take a break, your brain continues to mull things over, even if you aren't actively thinking about them.

So, take short breaks and go do something completely different for a few minutes. Your brain will thank you for it.

ASKING FOR HELP

Teachers are there to help you, and they *want* to help. If you're stuck on something or you're finding a particular activity really hard, ask for help. Don't ask before you've tried, though; attempt it first. But don't wait too long, either. It may be that you're just looking at something in the wrong way.

LEARNING STYLES

There was a trend a few years ago to analyze people's learning styles, to see whether they were "visual learners," who learn better using their eyes; "auditory learners," who learn better using their ears; or "kinesthetic learners," who learn better using their hands and via practical activities. It's true that you might find one or two of these methods more helpful, but they are not fixed aspects of who you are. Most people learn better with a combination of these methods. Practice in a way that suits you. Here are some suggestions you might try:

* Write in a variety of different-colored pens.

* Create pictures or posters to help you remember.

* Speak things aloud.

* Record what you want to learn and play it back.

* Walk while reciting the things you want to learn.

REWRITING AND SELF-TESTING

Rewriting and self-testing work particularly well, especially for things you've been reading and trying to understand. Some people make two mistakes when trying to understand and learn written material: they just read it over and over again, without taking it in properly, and they underline or highlight what they think are key points. These things don't usually work well! It's much better to rewrite and self-test.

Rewriting means putting something into your own words. The act of doing this helps you understand and remember the material because it's being processed by more parts of your brain than if you're simply reading it over and over. If you also keep asking yourself questions (self-testing), you should find this works even better. So, as you're reading something difficult, ask yourself a question, and then answer it in your own words.

126

For example, if you're reading something about the causes of the American Civil War or how the tides work, imagine someone is going to ask you to explain it to them. Have that in mind while you're reading, and then write your answer. Does it make sense? Check back and see if you got it right. All of these steps make it more likely that the information will go into your brain as understanding, not just as words on a page.

What if you've been practicing something wrong?

Just as practicing improves skills or knowledge by building pathways in the brain, it's also possible to create the wrong pathway by accidentally practicing something incorrectly. Suppose you hadn't been taught how to hold a tennis racket, or you picked up a violin and started trying to play it without lessons: you'd probably be doing it wrong. And the more times you did it wrong, the stronger these wrong pathways would become.

So, what's the answer? Get someone to teach you the correct way, and keep practicing, practicing, practicing! Soon you'll create the correct pathway, and the faulty one will become weaker and weaker. Simple!

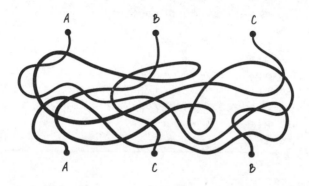

POSITIVELY YOU

A POSITIVE ATTITUDE

POSITIVELY HEALTHY

POSITIVELY BRAINY

POSITIVE ABOUT PEOPLE

A POSITIVE MOOD

POSITIVE BOOST

Using a dictionary (online or in print, but print might be easier), choose three words that you've never heard before. Learn how to spell them and what they mean. See if you can use them in your writing and speech over the next three days!

Research

PRACTICE AND LEARNING

How the brain learns
A simple video: www.youtube.com/watch?v=uqGz7uqoPZ4

Spaced learning
There's detail about Hermann Ebbinghaus and the "forgetting curve" here: www.growthengineering.co.uk/what-is-the-forgetting-curve /knowledgeplus.nejm.org/blog/spaced-repetition-the-most-effective -way-to-learn/

Interrupted tasks
Why taking breaks before you've finished a task may be better than waiting until you've finished, according to Bluma Zeigarnik: www .psychologistworld.com/memory/zeigarnik-effect-interruptions -memory

Use lots of areas of your brain

Each different type of thing you do uses different areas of your brain. If we could give you an MRI and ask you to do different activities—such as counting, reading, aiming, singing, recognizing faces, or imagining the color red—we would see different combinations of areas of your brain being active. If they are active, they are making and using connections.

If you spend a *lot* of time on one activity, you will grow more and stronger connections in the brain areas that activity uses. To become good at something—soccer, say, or playing the piano, or drawing faces—you need to grow as many strong connections as possible in the areas you need.

But there's another side to this: the areas you *don't* use tend to *lose* connections, or not grow in the first place. So you won't have those skills. If you learn a skill and then lose connections later, it's usually not too hard to grow them again. If you never had the skill in the first place, you can *usually* develop it later, but it's much harder.

Here's an example: suppose there's a girl and a boy. And suppose the girl learned Italian well when she was very young because her grandpa was Italian and he taught her. But the boy was never taught Italian. Then suppose the girl's grandpa dies when the girl is about seven, and she stops speaking Italian because her parents don't speak it. So, she had first built up a lot of connections in her brain for speaking Italian, but now she loses them because she doesn't keep the language skill.

Then, years later, when the girl and boy are adults, they both decide to learn Italian. The girl will find it easier than the boy because she still has many of those connections left, so she can more easily build them up again.

It's good to do lots of different things now, while you're young, to give yourself the best chance of developing the skills you want later. It doesn't matter if you stop after a few years: you've still built important connections that won't vanish completely.

You can't spend tons of time on *everything* because there are only a certain number of hours in the day, but you can make sure you do a wide variety of activities. Do things you enjoy— because you'll probably do better at them—but also challenge yourself. You can do it!

★ Using your brain

In your *Positively Teen* notebook, find a clean page and put today's date at the top. Then divide the page into the following sections. (I'm assuming it's a school day; if not, you can either wait till the next school day or adjust your notes to work for a holiday or weekend.)

Before lunchtime

During lunchtime

Afternoon until end of school

After school

On the way home from school

First part of the evening

Last part of the evening

Beneath each one, write what you did. At the end of the day, look at your activities. Were there lots of different types? Do you think you used many brain areas? Which of these were represented?

Physical activity

Music—listening or playing

Art, crafts, or making things

Talking

Reading

Writing

Numbers

Puzzles—general knowledge or problem-solving

Hobbies and relaxation

Speaking, reading, or listening to a foreign language

Something else I'm good at

Something else I find difficult

Working in a team

Thinking

Daydreaming

Using a screen

Resisting temptation

What could you add tomorrow to make sure you use lots of brain areas?

POSITIVELY YOU

A POSITIVE ATTITUDE

POSITIVELY HEALTHY

POSITIVELY BRAINY

POSITIVE ABOUT PEOPLE

A POSITIVE MOOD

Try new things— or do old things differently

When we try new things, our brain wakes up. Remember that chemical called dopamine? (I mentioned it when I talked about the "I is for INTEREST" part of FLOURISH on page 10.) I called it the "yes" chemical, and one of the things it says "yes" to is anything new. This is an important human trait: curiosity. If we are curious about things, we want to discover, explore, and know answers, and we are likely to find the answers and learn more. Being curious is a sign of intelligence and leads to all sorts of positive things.

To encourage us to be curious, our brains give us a little buzz of excitement (dopamine again) when we experience new things. Cultivate your curiosity! It could give you a burst of energy, a new way of seeing a problem, extra positivity, and exciting opportunities that you won't have if you keep your eyes closed.

Some ideas

Can you think of anything you'd like to try but never have? What's stopping you? Investigate it and see if you can try it now.

✳ Eat something you've never eaten. Try something strongly flavored, like a green olive, wasabi (careful—it's hot!), cilantro, lime juice, or Dijon mustard. Even if you don't like the taste, think about it seriously and try to describe it.

✳ Cook something you've never cooked before. If you've never cooked at all, try it! It's fun, easy, useful, and healthy. It not only helps inspire you while you're doing it, but it's a useful life skill. Start either by looking in the kitchen cupboards or fridge (ask your parents before taking something that might be designated for tonight's dinner!) or grabbing a recipe book or visiting a website for inspiration. It must be something you've never cooked before, such as vegan meringues, using the water from a can of chickpeas! (Check out the Internet for how to do this—you'll be amazed.)

✳ Challenge yourself to talk to a teacher you've never talked to at school. Ask them what book they are reading. If they aren't reading one, ask them why not.

✳ Ask if you can go on a family outing somewhere you've never been.

✳ Go to an art gallery and pretend you're a judge for an art prize. Buy a postcard of the work you decide is the best.

✳ Go to a museum and find out three facts you didn't know. Write them in your notebook.

✳ Pretend you're a tourist in the place where you live. Look at things through a tourist's eyes.

✳ Learn to say "hello," "good-bye," "please," "thank you," and "caterpillar" (or any random word you'd like to know) in a new language.

✳ If you're over sixteen, maybe you could take driver's ed! See if there's an organization near you that offers this.

Look at the list of hobbies (on pages 136 to 140) and choose one you've never tried.

Some ideas for doing old things differently

✳ Rearrange the furniture in your room.

✳ Brush your teeth with the hand you don't normally use.

✳ Fold your arms in the normal way, and then fold them with the opposite one on top.

✳ Try drawing a picture or writing with your "wrong" hand.

✳ Walk a different way to school or get on the bus at a different stop.

✳ Do your hair differently.

✳ Speak backward.

Have a hobby

There are lots of positive reasons to have a hobby. They give you a break from normal schoolwork; help take your mind off worries; help you develop new skills; exercise different parts of your brain; help you make new friends; and some even make money. Hobbies make us into more rounded, complete people, with a good balance in our lives. They can take your life in interesting new directions, and you just never know what might happen. Also, you don't have to take exams or tests in them (though sometimes you can), and if you don't enjoy your hobby, you can just stop doing it! What's not to like?!

When I was writing this book, I went onto my social media networks and asked a simple question to my friends who are parents: "What hobbies do your teens have?" I was astonished by the range of answers! I'm going to include them all here, for two reasons: first, so that you can have ideas that you might not have thought of (though some are more obvious); and second, because I want adults to stop saying, "Oh, teenagers—they just spend all their time on the Internet."

I've tried to divide the hobbies into categories, but there's some overlap. On YouTube you'll find videos to show you how to do whatever you're interested in.

Physical activities that usually need lessons or coaching and are mostly done in groups, teams, or clubs

Swimming—competitively or just for exercise

Diving

Scuba diving

Ice hockey

Hockey

Rugby

Soccer refereeing (You can earn money doing this, apparently.)

Ballet

Hip-hop or break dancing

Scottish/Highland/country dancing

Indian dancing—and other international dancing

Boy/Girl Scouts—various organizations for different ages around the world

Geocaching—great family activity

Gymnastics

Trampolining

Fencing—this is also great for people with dyspraxia, because they're not using both sides of their body in the same way at the same time. Several people mentioned that it's also great for those who find social situations difficult—the mask helps!

Martial arts

Circus school and aerial skills, such as silks, hoops, and dancing

Canoeing and rowing

Sailing

Skiing and snowboarding

Archery

Physical activities that may require lessons/coaching but can often be done solo or with friends

Climbing (indoor climbing center)—this was mentioned as especially great for people who like to work on their own, not in groups

Parkour

BMX and other biking

Dog training

Skateboarding

Go-karting

Horse riding—if you help out at the stables, it cuts the cost

Golf

Soccer

Baseball

Skating

POSITIVELY YOU

A POSITIVE ATTITUDE

POSITIVELY HEALTHY

POSITIVELY BRAINY

POSITIVE ABOUT PEOPLE

A POSITIVE MOOD

Bike riding

Going for walks

Bird-watching

Mental activities

Reading—on your own or
in book clubs at school, the library, or online

Computer coding

Electronics and robotics

Computer gaming—if it doesn't become an obsession that
occupies an unhealthy amount of time. "Unhealthy" would
be any amount of time that prevents you from having enough
physical and face-to-face social activity and doing your work.

Solving Rubik's Cubes

Puzzles, such as Sudoku

Science clubs

Bridge and other card games

Watching films and learning all the facts behind them

Becoming an expert—your chosen topic could be your
favorite band or celebrity, all the capital cities around the
world, someone from history, dinosaurs, your favorite author,
anything.

Creative activities

Writing—either on your own or in a club, at the library, or at school—maybe using Wattpad. You could keep a private journal or start a blog, which can be private or for a wider audience—ask your school librarian or teacher for advice about staying safe with this; or write stories and poems, either just for fun or aiming to be a published writer one day.

Art

Making Manga comics

Animation and moviemaking, including stop-motion animation

Photography

Playing musical instruments for orchestra or solo playing

Steel drums—I know this is part of the previous point, but I felt it deserved a mention!

Singing

Composing songs

Drama—either acting or working backstage, doing stage management or lighting or whatever

Baking and other cooking; sushi-making; chocolate-making

Sewing

Knitting, crochet, finger-knitting

Basket-making from local materials

Origami

Crafts; model-making from kits

Woodwork

Tie-dyeing

Pottery

Glass painting

POSITIVELY YOU

A POSITIVE ATTITUDE

POSITIVELY HEALTHY

POSITIVELY BRAINY

POSITIVE ABOUT PEOPLE

A POSITIVE MOOD

Things that can be "hobbies" or just good ways of passing the time and using different areas of the brain

(All the previous ideas can obviously also work like this, too—you don't have to have actual "hobbies," just things you enjoy doing.)

Nature and ecology, bugs and birds

Rummaging in the woods, making bows and arrows and carving things out of dead wood

Climbing trees

Gardening—this has been mentioned several times. You don't need a big garden. In fact, you don't need a garden at all. There are loads of things that can be grown in a pot on a windowsill, depending on where you live.

Bonsai—something to grow that doesn't need much space at all

Sunday school or other cultural club

4-H clubs

Fixing bikes and learning how machines work

Upcycling—turning used items into something else and selling or using them

Making beauty treatments

Volunteering for all sorts of charities, befriending the elderly

Collecting things—anything: egg cups, shells, wildflowers (don't dig anything up), coins, stamps, photos of sports stars

If you don't think those ideas are interesting enough, I was told about some more that were slightly too unusual to put in the main list: competitive sheep-shearing; competitive wood chopping; breeding sheep, alpaca, and angora rabbits; and sheepdog training! Those were from rural Australia, but you probably have some local activities and crafts where you live.

I hope adults are impressed by this. I'm exhausted. Go, positively teens!

POSITIVELY YOU

A POSITIVE ATTITUDE

POSITIVELY HEALTHY

POSITIVELY BRAINY

POSITIVE ABOUT PEOPLE

A POSITIVE MOOD

Control your screen use

Our screen-based devices such as laptops, tablets, and smartphones are amazing and powerful. They create huge opportunities to find out about anything in the world and to connect with other people of all backgrounds. Those are really important benefits that make your generation much more open-minded and knowledgeable than I was at your age. But there may be some problems with using screens too much—as many of us do.

Let's take a quick look at the possible problems, and then think how we can use our screens in more healthy and positive ways.

First, did you notice that I said "we"? That's because what I'm about to say applies equally to me and all the adults you know, as well as to you! Tell your parents that if you have to be careful about screen use, so do they, for exactly the same reasons. To be honest, I am quite unimpressed by the way some adults use their screens while telling you not to do so. If it's unhealthy for you, it's unhealthy for them as well. And they should set a good example.

DISTRACTION

Screens of all sorts (especially if connected to the Internet or other people) are distracting, and the science is clear on this. Research shows that even if someone next to us is on a laptop and we're not, we are usually slightly distracted by it. (The loss of concentration is measurable and can make us perform less well on a task.) Just having our phone in sight occupies a tiny bit of concentration so we focus less well on the task we're trying to do. And some studies suggest that if we read information on a screen, we comprehend and process and remember the information less well than if we had read it on paper. (The difference is small but something to think about. This seems to apply to all age groups, not just older people who didn't grow up with this technology.)

One problem is the fact that our screens bring lots of temptations: icons, ads, and links encouraging us to click on them. Our curious minds notice these distractions, and we spend a lot of brainpower deciding which to ignore and which to follow. There's a *lot* of evidence that this is all making many people less good at concentrating for a long period of time. I'm afraid there's also evidence that your age group is more distractible than teenagers used to be, even though you grew up with everything digital.

Screens usually force us to multitask, and almost no one is good at that. We might think we are, but we can't really do well on a high-concentration task if something else is occupying some of our brain "bandwidth." It's like trying to do something on a broadband line that is being used by someone streaming a video. Everything slows down and it doesn't work as well.

★ Quiz

You can find more detailed quizzes online, but this is a good start to discover if you have unhealthy Internet use. For each of these questions, answer: Never, Almost Never, Sometimes, Somewhat Often, or Very Often. These questions refer to social and pleasure use, when you use your screen-based device for personal, not work, reasons. And "online" includes anything you do on your mobile phone, Internet, or computer-game device.

★ How often do you find you've been online for longer than you intended?

★ How often do you find you don't have enough time for your schoolwork because you've been online?

★ When you're not online, are you thinking about the next time you can go online?

★ How often do you check your notifications (from social media, email, gaming community, and the like) before you start your homework?

★ Are you sometimes secretive about how much time you spend online?

★ Do you feel happier when you're online than when you're off-line?

★ Do you pick up your smartphone to avoid talking to people?

Score as follows:

Never = 0; Almost Never = 1; Sometimes = 2; Somewhat Often = 3; Very Often = 4

Your score:

First, note that if you scored 3 or 4 on a question, this should encourage you to change your behavior in this area.

0–7 You don't have a real problem with your screen use. (But see my point above.)

8–14 This is an acceptable score, though 13 and 14 are borderline. And, as above, a 3 or 4 score on any answer should alert you to take more care.

15+ Find ways to moderate your use, for the sake of your health, well-being, and work.

19+ It's very likely that you are using your devices in an unhealthy way, and you'd feel and function better if you were able to stay off-line more.

ADDICTION

These devices have some addictive aspects, in similar ways to things like sugar, tobacco, alcohol, and illegal drugs. This does *not* mean that everyone will become addicted, or that the addiction would be as dangerous as the others I mentioned. But it's so easy to find that we want to go online or play screen-based games more and more and more. If this means we aren't spending enough time on other things—such as schoolwork, getting outside for fresh air, and chatting with family and friends—that's a problem.

LOSING SKILLS?

Most of us have gained lots of skills and important knowledge through the Internet. But we may also be losing a few. Some people worry that our memory is getting worse because we don't usually need to remember things, now that we can so easily look anything up. I'm not sure about that, and I'm not even sure it matters, if it means we can do other things with our brains. The ancient Greeks worried that if people had things written down, they'd lose their memory, too, but we still seem to have pretty good brains.

There's one thing I do worry that some people are losing: the skill of talking. Making conversation is often hard; it requires practice and effort. But so often we just pull out a phone instead of talking to people. If I ruled the world, people would never have their phones on or visible while having a meal or spending time with someone. I love my phone and I am guilty of using it too much, but in-person interaction comes first.

Teenagers often tell me how annoying and upsetting it is when parents use phones when their kids want to talk to them. Unless it's a complete emergency, which it hardly ever is, that's not acceptable. You have my permission to tell them off!

Keep talking to people. It's an important skill for life, useful socially and for your careers. It's a fundamental human behavior and one that has contributed to our success. And it does take practice. If you avoid talking because it's so much easier to use your phone, you'll find it harder when you *need* to talk. You'll find ideas to help with this in POSITIVE ABOUT PEOPLE on page 151.

LOSING THINKING TIME

Any time we have five minutes waiting for a bus, many of us don't spend those minutes thinking or looking at the sky or trees: we get our phone out and check to see how many "likes" our latest social media post got. Of course that doesn't matter sometimes, but if it means we don't get any time just to enjoy our thoughts, I think that's an important loss.

I will talk about this much more in **Just think** on page 196.

A healthy balance

As I've said, there's nothing wrong with screens, but it becomes a problem when we use them too much. We might be missing out on other important things. It's the same with video games: there's nothing wrong with them, until we do them so much that we negatively affect our other activities or find it really hard to stop.

Somehow, we need to find a balance. There's no rule about how much or how little screen time is OK, but it has to be an amount that *feels* right and that allows us to do lots of other things, too.

Think about whether your screen use stops you from doing any of these things:

✷ Work—schoolwork, homework, whatever

✷ Friends—you might engage with friends on social media, but that isn't enough. Even quiet people benefit from seeing other people. (I'll talk about that in the next section.)

* Getting physical exercise and fresh air

* Eating and sleeping

* Hobbies and interests—some of this might be online; that's fine, but see the next point.

* Being off-line!

SWITCH OFF SCREEN (SOS) TIME

This should apply to the whole family; it can also work well at school, and if your school has SOS time, embrace this. You might moan about it with your friends, but if you're all doing it, it's easy! Notice how good it feels to be off-line for a while. At family mealtimes, actually talk to one another about your day, ask questions, get angry about something you heard in the news, discuss your next vacation or what you want to do over the weekend.

OUT OF SIGHT, OUT OF MIND

When you're working, make sure your phone is out of sight. Ideally, not in the same room. If it has to be in the room, have it completely switched off and in your bag.

APPS

There are apps to help you avoid the temptation of checking social media while working. You can set them so that they block just social media, email, or the whole Internet. I won't name any, as they keep changing, but you should be able to find a free one. Use it! You'll feel good, and you'll get your work done so much faster and better.

POSITIVELY YOU

A POSITIVE ATTITUDE

POSITIVELY HEALTHY

POSITIVELY BRAINY

POSITIVE ABOUT PEOPLE

A POSITIVE MOOD

POMODORO TECHNIQUE

This is a technique for time management, based on the simple idea of a kitchen timer. You can use a timer or a Pomodoro app. You choose an amount of time—twenty-five minutes is good, because it doesn't feel too long—set the timer, switch off or block social media, and work hard for that amount of time. The amazing thing is that when the timer pings, you usually want to keep on working! I know it sounds unbelievable, but it seems to let you get into the zone, and the feeling of working hard is so good that you want to keep it going.

IF/THEN STRATEGIES

This is a technique used to help people resist temptation. It's very simple, but very effective. You give yourself a rule, like this: "If I am tempted to check my Instagram feed, then I will drink a sip of water instead." You probably think I'm weird to suggest something so simple, but why not try it? There's good science behind it. It doesn't have to be a glass of water, but anything instead of the thing you want to resist. The good thing about a sip of water is that it's good for you, too. Double win!

POSITIVE BOOST

Switch off all screens now and see how you feel. If you've already done so, great! Notice the calm around you and the peace in your head. Notice the absence of that buzzing noise or the lights. Appreciate that for a little while no one can bother you or ask you anything. And you can switch back whenever you want, but for now just be chill and calm.

If you're wondering why I know so many of these strategies, it's because I, too, am very easily tempted to mess around on social media instead of working. So, I have armed myself with all these techniques. They really help!

Resources

CONTROLLING SCREEN USE

Distraction

Teen Ink: www.teenink.com/hot_topics/what_matters/article/781313/Digital-Distraction/

The *New York Times* on digital distraction: www.nytimes.com/2010/06/07/technology/07brain.html

Time magazine: time.com/money/3956968/cell-phone-alert-productivity/

Distraction from the laptop of the person next to you: www.rcinet.ca/en/2013/08/20/new-study-shows-computers-in-class-distract-both-users-and-non-users/

Having your phone in sight makes you focus less well on the task you're trying to do: psycnet.apa.org/index.cfm?fa=buy.optionToBuy&id=2014-52302-001

And: psmag.com/social-justice/presence-smart-phone-lowers-quality-person-conversations-85805

Digital natives seem not to be better at multitasking or dealing with distraction: phys.org/news/2016-01-digital-distraction-class.html

Reading on a digital device may make us comprehend, process, and remember less well than if we read it on paper: www.scientificamerican.com/article/reading-paper-screens/

Resisting temptation

Ideas to help us all manage our screen time well:

For parents: healthykidshealthyfuture.org/5-healthy-goals/reduce-screen-time/resources/

From the BBC: www.bbc.com/future/story/20131010-lose-the-phone-reclaim-your-life

You will notice that all the resources above involve using a screen and the Internet! I'm not saying there is anything wrong with *good* use of screens. You might also be interested in my book *The Teenage Guide to Life Online*, which goes into all this in much more detail.

Summing up

In this chapter, you've learned how practice makes you better at things, and what happens in your brain when you do it. You've seen how doing lots of different things will help grow different areas of your brain, and you've seen why trying new things and having hobbies creates variety and interest, making your brain more healthy. Finally, you've discovered the benefit of controlling your screen use.

You have so much power, so much potential, the possibility to control so much more than you might think: grow your brain positively, and it will repay you with success and confidence.

Positive About People

Humans are social creatures. We need friends and people to support us. As long as humans have existed, we've tended to work in pairs and groups. We have partners, families, friends, communities, clubs—all sorts of groups at school, work, and socially. Some of us like spending a lot of time with people and enjoy big groups. Some love spending time on our own, or with just one friend at a time. Often, which of these things we prefer depends on how we are feeling—and who the other people are!

People who enjoy time on their own—and I'm one of them—still need friends. We need to know whom we can turn to when we need help or we want to be with someone else. Psychologists know that networks and friendships are vital to our well-being. Not having anyone to turn to is a horrible feeling.

Sometimes it's easy to make friends. Other times it's harder. But friendships don't happen without our making an effort. A stranger won't turn up on the doorstep and say, "Will you be my friend?" (That would be a bit weird!) There are things we need to do to build bonds with people. So, to boost this part of your well-being, there are a few things to do.

POSITIVELY YOU

A POSITIVE ATTITUDE

POSITIVELY HEALTHY

POSITIVELY BRAINY

POSITIVE ABOUT PEOPLE

A POSITIVE MOOD

Talk face-to-face

Because of modern technology, we can so easily "talk" to people online, but talking face-to-face is still important for two main reasons.

First, it helps us build the friendships and support we need now or might need one day. Although we can start or continue a friendship online, with texts, social media, or other messages, there are advantages when we can see the other person and read his or her body language and facial expressions. It's easier to know what the other person is really thinking. Talking face-to-face keeps us connected to reality and stops us from living too much inside our own heads. (Spending time there is fine as long as we don't hide there excessively!)

Second, talking to people face-to-face teaches us a set of skills we'll need often during our lives, which we need to practice. The ability to talk to someone we don't know is incredibly powerful and opens doors, leading to new experiences, knowledge, and opportunities. So many jobs call for people who can get along with others.

Here are some examples of the times when the skill of talking to people will help you:

✳ In an interview

✳ In any job—especially one working with people, and that's most jobs

✳ When you want to persuade someone of your point of view

✳ When you move somewhere new—new school, job, or location

✳ When you have to walk into a room of strangers

✳ When you want to help a friend

✳ When you are trying to sort out problems between people

✳ When you want to be selected for something, such as a team or a play. If you've already engaged with someone by talking to them, they are more likely to pick you or notice you.

But it can be difficult to talk to people, can't it? It's so easy to send a quick text message or communicate through social media. And it's fine to do that sometimes: you're allowed to be on your own and have peace and quiet, some "me-time." I'm definitely someone who loves and needs to spend enough time alone. I'm an introvert, so, although I manage to enjoy social things, I get tired and stressed if I spend too much time with other people, even people I like.

I believe that making time to talk face-to-face with people gives us a more positive life. And it gets easier with practice. If you give yourself lots of opportunities to talk to people—of your own age and others—you'll gain skills that will help you throughout your life. You don't have to do anything special or difficult: just don't *avoid* face-to-face situations. Join in conversations when you can, and don't worry if you sometimes can't think of anything to say: listening is just as important in conversation as talking. In fact, the world would be a better place if people spent more time listening!

153

It's perfectly OK to be a quiet or shy person. These are not problems. But they do mean you might need to try extra hard and make sure you don't hide behind your smartphone. Be proud every time you join in a conversation and realize that you're doing yourself some good. Gradually, it will get easier, and you'll learn to act more confidently.

Ideas for starting conversations

✳ Ask a question: "Where did you get your jacket?" "What do you think of the geography teacher?" "Did you watch *The Voice*?"

✳ Make eye contact—actual eye contact, not a quick glance at someone's forehead. Just for a few seconds—anything more is staring! This can be incredibly hard for some people, and you might have to force yourself, but I promise it will get easier. Practice on your family.

✳ Simple situations like buying something in a shop or ordering a drink can give you opportunities to use eye contact, a smile, and a few words.

✳ Smile—again, not too much, and not at inappropriate times!

✳ Look interested. Don't keep looking away and fidgeting when someone is talking.

✳ Plan topics to talk about in advance. If you've seen an amazing thing online or heard a weird story, store it in your mind until the right moment.

Social anxiety—sometimes called social phobia

Although it's quite natural to be shy and to find it difficult to talk to people, for a few people this is a huge problem that goes way beyond normal shyness. People who have a form of social anxiety (including selective mutism, where people sometimes find it impossible to get words out) may feel extreme stress and even panic when they have to interact with others. If this applies to you, there is help for you. Ask someone about seeing a doctor, who can direct you toward treatment. You can also find online support groups for your age, but seeing a doctor is still important.

Resources

SHYNESS AND SOCIAL ANXIETY

From *Psychology Today*: *https://www.psychologytoday.com/us/blog /surviving-your-childs-adolescence/201106/adolescence-and-shyness*

Anxiety BC: *www.anxietybc.com/parenting/social-anxiety-disorder*

Very Well Family: *https://www.verywellfamily.com/how-to-help-a -shy-teen-build-self-confidence-2611009*

POSITIVELY YOU

A POSITIVE ATTITUDE

POSITIVELY HEALTHY

POSITIVELY BRAINY

POSITIVE ABOUT PEOPLE

A POSITIVE MOOD

Value good friendship

Friendships can be among the best things in our lives, but they can also cause stress. Teenagers tend to rely on friends more than when they were younger. You may not want to talk to your parents about the things you used to talk about, so friends become even more important. Who you hang out with, and who "accepts" you, becomes part of your identity and how you see yourself, and very much affects your self-esteem.

When friendships go wrong, or when you are finding it hard to fit in, it can feel like the worst thing in the world. Feeling excluded is a horrible experience that most people can identify with if they think about it. This can be deliberate or completely unintentional.

I've written a lot about friendships—the good and the bad—in *The Teenage Guide to Friends* and on my website. I offer you four of the most important tips here.

✳ **1. If your friendships are going wrong or if you're finding it difficult to make friends, see this as a temporary phase.** Everything changes, especially at your stage of life. It's horrible now, but it will get better. There are more friends for you out there. Try not to let it color your opinion of yourself: it's just unfortunate that you haven't found the people you gel with yet. Very often, the people around you are just wrapped up in their own problems, which can make them selfish. They are most likely not putting themselves in your shoes, as they just don't have the headspace.

✳ **2. There's no prize for having *the most* friends.** One or two good friends are all you need. Don't worry that some people seem to have lots of friends: too many friends can be a problem—you can't really maintain close or strong relationships with so many. Focus on one or two people you feel comfortable with; being relaxed with friends is really important and will allow you to make the most of the relationships as well as show your best side.

✳ **3. Be good to your friends** (but don't let them abuse your generosity). Show them you like them; thank them when they help you; share their happiness when something great happens to them; treat them just as you'd like them to treat you.

✳ **4. Be good to yourself.** If someone doesn't make you feel comfortable, do they deserve to be your friend? Trusting people is good, but not if they keep hurting you. So, if there's someone who is supposed to be your friend but who you feel often manipulates you, always gets their own way, and seems always to think of themselves much more than you, consider whether it might be better to walk away gently from the friendship. They could be what we call a "toxic" friend or a "frenemy." You don't have to stay with them if it's hurting you.

Resources

VALUE GOOD FRIENDSHIPS

My book *The Teenage Guide to Friends* has sections on making friends, keeping friends, and walking away if it's not working for you.

A reassuring resource for teens: *www.best-friends-forever.com/friend-issues.html*

From *Scientific American*, "How to Deal with Frenemies": *www.scientificamerican.com/article/fickle-friends/*

POSITIVELY YOU

A POSITIVE ATTITUDE

POSITIVELY HEALTHY

POSITIVELY BRAINY

POSITIVE ABOUT PEOPLE

A POSITIVE MOOD

Trust caring adults

Babies and young children—as with young animals of any sort—have to rely on the adults close to them, whose job it is to keep them safe, fed, warm, and loved, and to teach them what they need to know. It's hard work being a new parent, but it's also rewarding and exciting.

Most parents and caregivers do a great job, often helped by other relatives and supported by teachers who also look after the child. Some parents and caregivers struggle more than others, maybe through physical or mental illness or all sorts of pressures, so some children don't have the early support and love they need and deserve.

As you become a teenager, your relationship with the adults around you often changes, especially with the adults closest to you. Sometimes, you want to be more independent and do things for yourself. Or you may disagree with what some of the adults around you say or be *really* irritated by them! Being irritated by your parents or caregivers is very normal. Sometimes, you might have arguments and maybe say things you don't really mean, and they might do the same.

POSITIVELY YOU

A POSITIVE ATTITUDE

POSITIVELY HEALTHY

POSITIVELY BRAINY

POSITIVE ABOUT PEOPLE

A POSITIVE MOOD

There might also be times when you question whether you love your parents. Again, this is quite normal and natural. It can feel horrible at the time, but arguments and negative feelings do not mean that you or they are horrible people.

Relationships between parents and teenagers can be rocky for a while, but once you've gone through this period, all is usually well. When you're feeling negative toward someone, try not to let that become bigger in your mind than is necessary. Focus on being the best that you can, and keep your mind on the things you can control.

Young children usually go to their parents or caregivers for help, but you might prefer not to share particular concerns with your parents and will probably want a range of adults to support you. That's OK. It's important to know whom you can go to for help and reassurance. This is about knowing who your "trusted adults" are. They can be different people for different situations. Sometimes, it might be your parents. You might also go to a teacher. Schools usually have a teacher who is assigned to student support or guidance; there should be someone in the school whose job it is to help. But you can go to *any* teacher. Even if teachers don't know how to help with every situation themselves, they are trained in how to respond and get you the right help.

Resources

TRUSTED ADULTS

Your Life Your Voice has a page called "Have a problem talking to your parents?": *www.yourlifeyourvoice.org/Pages/tip-problem-talking-to-your-parents.aspx*

Grow your empathy

Empathy is the ability to deeply understand what another person is feeling. We sometimes use the phrase "walk a mile in someone else's shoes" to describe how we try to understand someone else. No one has perfect empathy, but it's incredibly helpful if we can have as much as possible, and it's important to try to develop it.

If we don't understand how the people around us are feeling, we might say the wrong things. If we do understand, we have a better idea of how to react. Empathy is one thing that helps us become effective humans, able to work well with others, but it also makes others behave better toward us. If we have strong empathy skills, we usually find it easier to make friends, especially if the people around us have good empathy skills, too.

How do we develop empathy?

Most humans start to develop empathy naturally between the ages of three and four. At that age, we start to realize that what someone else feels or thinks might not be how we are feeling or thinking. This is called Theory of Mind, the idea that your mind is different from mine, that we may know, believe, think, and feel different things. Then we gradually start to learn *how* particular events or situations make people feel, and we can begin to guess what someone else might be feeling.

For example, we learn that if a pet dies, someone will be sad because they loved the pet. We learn that winning a prize usually makes someone feel fantastic, but if they have to walk up onto the stage they might also feel embarrassed and shy, or they might feel really proud, or a mixture. We learn that different people have different reactions.

How do we learn this? In two ways: first, by experiencing it ourselves, and second, by listening to how people describe their feelings when they tell the story of their experience.

In fact, reading or hearing stories—true or made-up—are wonderful ways of growing empathy skills. Storytelling is something humans have done for many thousands of years, since long before written language. And many experts believe that the *reason* this habit and skill developed was because being able to understand how others think and feel is an incredibly powerful way to build connections, teams, and groups. When we work together and share things, we can achieve so much more, and empathy helps us work together. (Working on our own is also important, but if we do an amazing piece of work on our own and we have no one to share it with later, that wouldn't be as useful or satisfying.)

★ An empathy exercise

Think of someone you know who has a very different life from yours in some way. Maybe they have much more or less money, or a different family set-up, or are different from you in any number of other ways. Don't write their name down.

★ Write down one to three things that are different about their life compared to yours.

★ Write down one thing you think makes them luckier than you. Write down how this might make them *feel*.

★ Write down one thing that makes them unluckier. Write down how this might make them *feel*.

★ Imagine it is the person's birthday. What do they feel?

★ Imagine the person has just done badly on a test. What do they feel?

★ How do you feel when it's your birthday?

★ How do you feel when you've done badly on a test?

★ Are your feelings exactly the same as the other person's, or not exactly? Why do you think that is?

You might have exactly the same feelings, but it's more likely that you won't. If the other person has different things going on in their lives, their reactions and emotions will probably be a little different from yours. Not definitely, but probably. It's good to remember that. We can't be 100 percent sure what someone else is feeling, but we can do our best to guess.

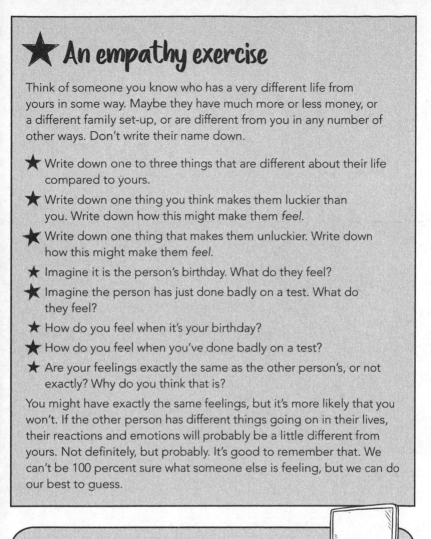

Resources

GROWING EMPATHY

EmpathyBomb: *http://empathybomb.com*

Do things for others

Doing a good deed for someone else boosts our own mood and improves our sense of well-being. There's plenty of research about this. It gives us a warm feeling and raises self-esteem. It builds friendships. It also makes it more likely that the person will do something for us, though that isn't why we do it.

Doing things for others but never being thanked, or being ignored or taken for granted, does *not* make us feel better, of course. People should be grateful when another person helps them, but if they are very upset, they might simply not have the headspace to recognize that someone has helped them. That's understandable.

I'm not suggesting you do things for other people and never think of yourself. You have to think of yourself, too. But try doing some things to help friends or people who need it, and you'll feel better. And the actions don't have to be big, either.

Ideas

✳ Hold the door open for an older person and smile at them.

✳ Do a chore at home without being asked.

✳ Give someone in your family a hug.

✳ Offer to do small tasks for a neighbor who needs help: taking letters to mail, weeding their garden, doing a little bit of shopping.

✳ Bake a cake for someone's birthday or to say thank you, sorry, or good luck.

✳ Make a homemade card for a friend.

POSITIVE BOOST

Invite a friend or two to go for ice cream or to the movies. As soon as possible! If the weather forecast is good for the weekend, plan a picnic. Whatever you choose, it will be something to look forward to.

Resources

DOING THINGS FOR OTHERS

Research into how doing a good deed for someone else boosts our mood and improves well-being: *sonjalyubomirsky.com/files/2012/09 /Lyubomirsky-Layous-20132.pdf*

The Random Acts of Kindness website has lots of ideas and stories about this activity and its benefits: *www.randomactsofkindness.org*

Summing up

This section has revealed how the people around us make a difference to our lives and sense of well-being. Building good relationships, among both those in your age group and the adults who care about you, will help your self-esteem and create a good network of people to have fun with, to share your life with, and to support you when you need it. And you've seen that learning the skills of talking to people you don't know well is really worthwhile, helping you now and throughout your life. Face-to-face communication is important, but it can be difficult, so we sometimes need to drag ourselves away from our smartphones and make the effort to practice the skills of eye contact and face-to-face conversation.

You've learned about the value of empathy, of doing your best to understand what someone else might be feeling. And remember how making someone else feel good helps make you feel good, too. Good relationships are about thinking both of what other people need and what we need ourselves, so try to ignore any negative people around you, people who drag you down, and focus on building relationships with positive people. And smile. There's a phrase, "Smile and the whole world smiles with you." I think it's a pretty good way of thinking.

A Positive Mood

Mood is different from a sense of well-being. Well-being, as you know, is about having generally good mental and physical health. Mood is about how you feel right now.

What kind of mood are you in at this moment? Start by thinking generally: good mood, bad mood, or neither.

Then think in a bit more detail. Good, or positive, moods will usually make you feel happy, excited, proud, pleased, relaxed, comfortable, thrilled, content, or alert. Negative moods will usually mean you feel worried, scared, sad, upset, shocked, devastated, undermined, low, numb, angry, disgusted, confused, or stressed.

Sometimes we know why we're in a particular mood, but sometimes we don't. We can feel happy or sad without knowing why.

★ Analyze your mood

You might like to analyze your mood in more detail.

Get your notebook and write down the date and time of day.

★ Write whether your mood right now is positive, negative, or neither.

★ Write as many words as you can think of to describe your feelings in more detail. You don't have to write sentences, just words that come to mind.

★ Write whether you know *why* you feel like that. Did something just happen to you, or did someone say something? Did you just wake up feeling like this, or did it happen during the day? Is this your usual mood, or is it unusual?

★ You could do the same tomorrow or one day next week. See if there's any difference. Notice how things that people say or things that happen affect your mood.

Some things that affect mood are outside our control. I think it's helpful and positive to acknowledge those, so we don't spend time worrying about them. On the other hand, even if we can't stop things from happening, we can sometimes take action to improve our mood, anyway.

Here are some things we can't control:

⁕ **Weather!** Usually, a warm or sunny day lifts people's moods, while a cold gray day does the opposite, especially if we have to go outside. A cold wind often makes me angry. Even though we obviously can't control the weather, we can stop letting it affect us too negatively. We can find fun things to do indoors; we can make sure we wear warm enough clothes; we can do tasks we've been putting off.

168

✱ **Hormones**. Hormones are chemicals that regulate all sorts of things, including appetite, sleep, and growth. During adolescence, everyone experiences big increases in the hormones that are turning them into adults of whichever gender. These hormones can have a major effect on mood, making us feel sad or angry or easily irritated or excited. Many (but not all) girls notice this because of monthly cycles of hormones, while male hormones don't undergo monthly cycles, so the differences are less obvious. But both male and female hormones can be responsible for big mood swings. (If this affects you in a major way, a doctor will be able to give you good advice.)

✱ **Things that happen to us**. These might be big or small things, but they will often affect our moods. It's just natural.

There are usually steps we can take to stop these factors from affecting us too negatively or for too long. The ideas that follow will help you keep your mood as positive as possible. But don't worry if you sometimes feel down: it's completely normal and natural. It's part of being human. What we need are ways to keep those low feelings in their place: temporary and manageable.

Spot your signs of stress

Although stress isn't a "mood," having too much stress can certainly lower our mood. If we can spot signs of stress, we can use simple strategies to improve mood and well-being.

Stress is really important. Without it, we'd lie around all day and never push ourselves to do well! When there's any need to react to a difficult or dangerous situation, or any challenge, our brain triggers the chemicals adrenaline and cortisol to race around our body. These make our hearts beat faster, pushing more blood (with oxygen and glucose) to where we need it: the muscles of legs and arms, for example, to make us run faster or jump higher. And our "nervous system" is also activated, helping us focus on the challenge at hand and ignore irrelevant things.

This gives us the chance to perform well. So, stress can be good!

The trouble is, we can also have too much of it. This causes two main problems:

★ Too much adrenaline can make us feel panicky. Then we are more likely to make mistakes or freeze.

★ Cortisol builds up in our system. Adrenaline disappears quickly once a challenge is over, but cortisol hangs around. So, if you have more stress soon after the first rush, there's still cortisol from the earlier time. And after a while, the buildup can lead to major problems: difficulty sleeping; poor concentration and focus; being vulnerable to minor illnesses, such as colds; bad moods; irritability. All of this adds up to lower well-being.

How do you know if you're suffering from too much stress? Not everyone reacts the same, but here are some common symptoms:

✷ Lots of headaches or stomachaches

✷ Often feeling dizzy or light-headed—this can also be from not eating enough food, so think about that first.

✷ Feeling sick

✷ Appetite changes—this might be having no appetite, or it might be feeling hungry all the time, or perhaps craving the wrong food.

✷ Poor sleep—you might find it hard to get to sleep or wake up often or early. Almost everyone experiences this sometimes, but if it's happening a lot, this is a possible sign of stress.

✷ Compulsive habits—biting nails, pulling hair, picking skin

✷ Eczema

✷ Feeling anxious without quite knowing why

✷ Being snappy and irritable and finding it hard to control your temper or manage your anger

Understand that these symptoms can be signs of something else, even though it's unlikely to be anything serious. If you experience any of them for more than a couple of weeks, see a doctor so that other illnesses can be ruled out. But these symptoms are very likely to be caused by stress.

Once you know how *you* react to stress, you can spot symptoms early, then take steps to prevent it from getting worse. In that way, you'll have better control over your well-being and performance.

One important thing: being stressed is not a sign of weakness! It's completely natural, just like the symptoms of a cold or flu. Trying to ignore it is not the best way to have great well-being. My motto is: "Know about it, notice it, nail it!"

★ How I feel

Not everyone has the same signs of stress. This activity will help you begin to notice how stress tends to affect *you* and *your* body. If you are feeling very relaxed and positive at the moment, you probably won't notice any of the symptoms in the list below—great! Instead, think of a time when you did feel worried, anxious, or sad and see if you can remember how it made you feel. Then you can learn to spot the signs early and take steps to relax.

In your notebook, draw a picture of yourself. Your picture doesn't have to be perfect: we just want to see where your head, arms, and legs are!

Make a list of any of the following things you tend to notice when life is difficult or causing anxiety. Add any others you can think of. Shade in or highlight the parts of your body where you experience these things:

Frequent headaches

Unexplained stomach pains

Dizziness and feeling faint

Tight feeling in chest as though it's hard to take a full breath

Heart seems to be beating very fast.

Feeling sick/nauseous

Jaw or face feels very tight.

Muscles in neck, shoulders, and jaw are tight.

Biting fingers or chewing lip

Breathing feels high up in chest, not low down.

Feeling panicky

Sweating a lot

Being extra clumsy

Not being able to concentrate

Sleeping badly

Twitching muscle near eye

Itchy skin or eczema

These are all normal experiences, and they don't do you any harm on their own, but they interfere with your sense of enjoyment and can build up to make you too ill to work and achieve your best. By spotting the signs early, then following my advice in this chapter and the rest of the book, you can have the best possible control of your well-being.

POSITIVELY YOU

A POSITIVE ATTITUDE

POSITIVELY HEALTHY

POSITIVELY BRAINY

POSITIVE ABOUT PEOPLE

A POSITIVE MOOD

POSITIVE BOOST

When you're feeling tense, notice whether your breathing seems high in your chest or lower down. Focus on shifting your breathing downward so that your belly moves when you breathe, not your upper chest. Let your stomach muscles completely relax, flopping outward. Notice how much more relaxed you feel, immediately. You'll find detailed instructions online if you search "belly-breathing." There's also a free audio on my website and in the **Resources** below.

Resources

SIGNS OF STRESS

My website has lots of advice, and resources for schools, parents, and teens. There is a lot of detailed advice in my book, *The Teenage Guide to Stress*, and I have classroom resources for schools to teach these important skills: *www.nicolamorgan.com*

From Kids Health: *kidshealth.org/en/teens/stress.html*

From *Psychology Today*: *https://www.psychologytoday.com/us/blog/teen-angst/201109/teen-stress-how-much-is-too-much*

From Psycom: *https://www.psycom.net/hidden-signs-teen-anxiety*

From Mind: *www.mind.org.uk/information-support/tips-for-everyday-living/stress/signs-of-stress/*

Manage your environment

Do you have a space that's your own? Your own bedroom would be perfect, of course, but if you share a bedroom, you can still have an area that's yours, even if it's just your bed and desk. Your space needs to work for you, no one else, so think about whether there's anything you'd like to change. Surroundings can make a big difference to mood, and even small changes can have major results.

Do you *like* your space? How does it make you feel when you're in it? Safe, comfortable, relaxed, happy? Or annoyed, uncomfortable, stressed, negative? Even if you love your space, you might get some ideas from the list that follows.

Ideas

Colors matter. Different colors can create different moods. For example, red and orange tend to make us feel excited or even anxious, rather than relaxed. Blue tends to be more relaxing, but of course there are lots of shades of blue (or any other color), from bright to soft, and dark to pale. It's really about what you like and what makes you feel the way you want to. If you don't like the color in your room, maybe you could help repaint it? Maybe you could get a new duvet cover? Or put some things away and just keep the ones that are your chosen colors?

Messy room, messy mind? Actually, some people are genuinely fine with having a messy room, and maybe that's you (even if it isn't your parents!). But think carefully: do you feel more relaxed, in control, and positive when your room is untidy or tidy? If you'd really prefer a tidy space, but have let the mess build up, it could be time for a big cleanup. You'll feel better.

Why not ask an adult for help? That might seem like a really weird suggestion, but you would be surprised at how positively parents react if you ask in the right way. (Tip: you still have to do most of the work! You're just asking for help, not delegating the whole task.)

Place to work. Some people like to work at a desk, while others prefer sitting on the floor. Do you have the best working space for yourself? Or you might have two spaces: a desk for writing, and your bed or a pillow for reading. If you're working at a desk, you need a comfortable, adjustable chair, which doesn't have to be expensive. You need a good light in the right position so it doesn't make a shadow across your work. All this will help you feel better when you're working.

Some people notice a difference when facing a wall, window, or door while working. Experiment with what works for you.

176

Feng shui. This was very fashionable about twenty years ago. Whole books were written about it. Feng shui is the art of arranging a room so that positive energy is created. Even though it sounds odd, there are some good points. There are two things I think *can* make a difference: not having to step around items, and not having a door behind us when we work.

You can test this for yourself: try putting your chair right in the path between the door and your bed and see how tense it makes you! And try positioning your desk so that you are sitting with your back to the door: you'll probably find it makes you nervous and alert, thinking that someone might come in without your noticing.

The main point is that it can make a difference where you put furniture. Be aware of this and experiment as much as you can. Aim to feel comfortable and secure.

Resources

EFFECTS OF COLOR

Color psychology, the possible effects of different colors: *www.verywell.com/color-psychology-2795824*

Research on the color red, particularly suggesting that red causes people to react with greater speed and force: *https://www.ncbi.nlm .nih.gov/pubmed/21500913*

Positive about music

Music can be a great way to affect your mood. If you want to be full of energy and raise your mood, choose faster, livelier music. If you want to relax and wind down, especially leading up to bedtime, choose slower, gentler music. Not everyone will have exactly the same reaction.

If you don't *like* the music, it probably won't have a positive effect on your mood. So, choose music that helps *you* achieve the mood you're looking for.

There are other relaxing sounds, too, such as birdsong or whale song. You can find free audio recordings of these on the Internet.

Can you listen to music while you work?

Parents and teachers ask me this a lot, and they usually believe you *shouldn't* work while listening to music. I understand why they think so. But I've looked into the science and thought carefully about this. Based on that, my answer is: if you want to and you find it helps you concentrate, it's usually fine to do it.

Here's why. In theory, listening to music does occupy some of your brain "bandwidth," or thinking space. Everything does. So, in theory, that leaves a little bit less for concentrating on your work. But there are two reasons why listening to music while you work can still be a good idea:

1. Some noises can be very irritating: noises of your family somewhere in the house, of a TV next door, of other students in your classroom making noises with their pens or feet or sniffing. Sniffing is one of the *most* annoying things! And being irritated by something occupies a *lot* of brain bandwidth. So those noises can be terrible for concentration. Playing some music (when you're allowed to) blocks out those sounds and helps concentration.

2. You might have worries or thoughts buzzing around your head when you're trying to work. Playing music can then be helpful for getting "into the zone." Just as music can block out other sounds, it can also block out the "noise" inside your head.

Choose your music carefully if you want to work well, though. It needs to be familiar to you; otherwise you'll be concentrating on the music too much. I play the same music over and over when I'm writing because I would never try new music if I want to concentrate. You might find it easier to concentrate if the music has no lyrics, so that you won't be listening to the words. But I find that doesn't affect me if I'm familiar with the songs.

179

POSITIVELY YOU

A POSITIVE ATTITUDE

POSITIVELY HEALTHY

POSITIVELY BRAINY

POSITIVE ABOUT PEOPLE

A POSITIVE MOOD

However, some research suggests that if you're doing tasks that involve memorizing facts or lists you will not benefit from having music in the background.

One thing to be careful of: you can't listen to music during a test or exam. So, you don't want to get too used to working with music. Make sure you sometimes work without. If people are annoying you with their noises in an exam or even in class, consider wearing earplugs (but not when your teacher is talking to you!). I think earplugs are a great idea for exams.

Resources

BENEFITS OF LISTENING TO MUSIC

An article aimed at parents, on the benefit for teens of listening to music of their choice: www.livestrong.com/article/515082-how-does-music-affect-teenagers-emotions/agers

Mood changing music: mamiverse.com/how-types-of-music-genres-affect-mood-64945/

Music while you work—this article in the Guardian newspaper makes some useful points: www.theguardian.com/education/2016/aug/20/does-music-really-help-you-concentrate

Separating the tasks that may be positively affected and those that may be negatively affected: www.qsleap.com/articles/listening-music-studying-good-bad/

Does listening to music make you smarter? (Probably not.) www.psychologytoday.com/blog/your-musical-self/201005/the-mozart-effect-doesnt-work

A sense of sight

While we are thinking about mood, we should remember that what we see affects how we think and feel.

Sight is the most important and strongest sense for most humans, though, of course, people with impaired sight find other ways to experience the world and may have impressive other senses.

Here are a few things you might think about adding to your life to give you positive experiences through your eyes.

A natural view

A great way to get a mood boost through your eyes comes from looking at nature—particularly green spaces and big spaces. There's a lot of research about the benefits of looking at a beautiful natural view. Scientists have discovered that hospital patients tend to heal more quickly if they can see beautiful scenery, even in a picture or a mural. More research shows that being able to see green space outside your bedroom or house also improves mood.

But what if you live in a city? Go outside every day, and make sure you see some natural scenery, whether it's the green space of a park, the sea, or mountains in the distance. Every city has something to offer. Ask for a family trip over the weekend.

Research also suggests that we can have more creative ideas outside, or in a very high-ceilinged room, than indoors or under a low ceiling. So, get outside. Look at the sky, look at anything natural, and breathe the air!

POSITIVE BOOST

You don't have to be religious to be amazed by the brilliance of a cathedral, church, mosque, or temple. The high ceilings, windows, and statues are often incredible. Take a look and wonder at how people hundreds of years ago could have built them. The same applies to many ancient buildings. Just go and look: you'll be amazed.

Picture-perfect

You can alter your mood by looking at different pictures. It's obvious, really: looking at sad or frightening things will make us feel sad or frightened; looking at happy or fun things will lift our spirits. So, to feel more upbeat, find something that makes you feel happy to look at: a photo of a great vacation or something you did with your friends; a picture of kittens or puppies or baby lions or the sun or your sports hero. Whatever makes you smile inside.

Resources

BENEFITS OF NATURE

Lots of benefits are mentioned here, with references: *greatergood.berkeley.edu/article/item/how_nature_makes_you_kinder_happier_more_creative*

The effects of living by the sea on well-being: *www.ecehh.org/research-projects/does-living-by-the-coast-improve-health-and-well-being/*

Natural environments help our attention span: *journals.sagepub.com/doi/pdf/10.1111/j.1467-9280.2008.02225.x*

Green spaces may improve children's learning: *http://www.pnas.org/content/112/26/7937.full*

Images of nature help people who are in pain: *www.clemson.edu/cafls/vincent/articles/effects_of_nature_images.pdf*

Sensible scents

Some people are not particularly affected by smell, but for others it can be mood-changing. And it's quite easy to create something that has a smell you like. There are certain smells that make me go "Mmm" (yes, out loud). A few minutes before I wrote this, my neighbor brought me a bunch of sweet peas from his garden, and they are in my office right now—they have one of the best smells!

I use scented candles when I'm working or when I want to create a relaxed and warm mood at home. You might have something quite ordinary that you love the smell of—strawberries, banana, lemon, a particular soap, the smell of clean clothes, chocolate—and you could keep it with you when you work. And often that *is* something you could take into an exam. Obviously, some things work better for that than others, but you can use your imagination and problem-solving skills to find a way to have your favorite smells with you when you want them. You might have a scented scented eraser or pen that you love, for example.

Laughter medicine

You might think you can only laugh if you're already in a good mood, but in fact, laughing can *put* you in a good mood! Obviously, you have to find something to make you laugh, but with YouTube and all the hilarious videos out there, it should be fairly easy to find your favorites quickly. I love what appears when I search "goats screaming like humans," "dogs talking like humans," and "babies eating lemons." "Babies laughing" also produces excellent results because laughter is contagious: it's very hard to remain gloomy when babies are laughing.

But what's happening, and why does laughter work so well? It turns out that the muscles we use for smiling and laughing trigger the brain into producing chemicals called endorphins, which people often call "happy chemicals," because that's how they make us feel. They also take away pain.

Lots of people I know have particular comedy DVDs they will always watch when they need cheering up. It's a very good, simple way to give your mood a boost.

POSITIVELY YOU

A POSITIVE ATTITUDE

POSITIVELY HEALTHY

POSITIVELY BRAINY

POSITIVE ABOUT PEOPLE

A POSITIVE MOOD

Resources

EFFECTS OF SMILING

From *Psychology Today*: www.psychologytoday.com/blog/cutting
-edge-leadership/201206/there-s-magic-in-your-smile

Be engaged

Here's something interesting that can make a difference to your mood and therefore affect your well-being. Are you sometimes so involved in something that you don't notice the time? So into a game or a book that you don't notice someone enter or leave the room, don't hear the person talking to you, completely forget whatever else you're supposed to be doing?

This is called "engagement" or being in "flow." And psychologists believe it's really important to our well-being to have enough periods like this.

Do you also know that feeling when you can't concentrate on what you're trying to do, can't get into a book, keep being distracted and delaying your work because you're just not interested enough in it? That's a very common and annoying state of mind—quite stressful, in fact. You want to get your work done or you want to switch off from your whirling thoughts, but the tiniest things distract you. Every sound from people nearby seems loud and designed to irritate you. Even if the people near you aren't making a noise, you still *feel* their presence and you can't ignore them. This is the opposite of engagement.

187

So, how can we get into a state of engagement? There are many possible activities. I think they have to be things that need a lot of concentration, occupying a lot of what I like to call brain "bandwidth."

To understand this idea, think of computer or Internet capacity or speed, and how, if something is occupying a lot of available "bandwidth," other things happen more slowly. Our brains work similarly: if something is occupying a significant amount of our mental processing capacity, there's less left over for other things, and we work more slowly, less efficiently.

To get into a state of engagement, we need to do something that uses a lot of bandwidth, so we can be fully occupied. Here are some things I can think of that could work well. You might think of more. Remember that whatever it is, it has to be something you *want* to do and are interested in.

✳ Reading—anything you're interested in; fiction or nonfiction, short or long; graphic novels

✳ Investigating something on the Internet—again, it needs to be something you are really interested in.

✳ Making something difficult—a complicated model, for example

✳ A puzzle—Sudoku or a difficult crossword

✳ A card game where you have to think hard

✳ Learning a poem by heart

✳ Learning to do something new

✳ Playing a musical instrument or singing

✳ Any physical activity you love and are trying to succeed in

✳ Watching your favorite sports team

✳ A treasure hunt

✳ Acting

* Almost any hobby you really enjoy

* Something with a goal or target

* Video or computer games (caution: these can be so engaging that you can be tempted to do them too much.)

* Practicing or making a speech

* Anything you find difficult but enjoyable

* Anything that needs concentration, but you are interested in the result

* Your schoolwork, if it's something you're interested in

* Meditation

You might wonder why I haven't included television. That's because generally it doesn't occupy much brain bandwidth. Sometimes it does, when it's a program that grips you, but for most television, not much effort is required. The point about engagement is that it require some effort, some concentration.

It can be difficult to get into this state of engagement, so don't worry if you find it hard. Everyone struggles with this sometimes. But there are some ways we can help ourselves. When you want to concentrate on something, the three most important things include:

* Know what your goal is and why you're doing it. It could be that you want to read for half an hour for relaxation. Or it could be that you want to get your homework done quickly and well.

* Give yourself the best chance of not being disturbed. You might need to put a sign on your bedroom door or ask your parents for support.

* Remove the distraction of your phone or the Internet. If you must do something online, disable your social media accounts (see page 147).

POSITIVELY YOU

A POSITIVE ATTITUDE

POSITIVELY HEALTHY

POSITIVELY BRAINY

POSITIVE ABOUT PEOPLE

A POSITIVE MOOD

Don't worry about how many times you manage to feel engaged each day—there's no rule. Just look for opportunities and notice how great it feels when you do get "into the zone" and away from distractions of thoughts or external noises. (Read **Just think** on page 196, because this will take the pressure off if you can't always concentrate.)

Resources

ENGAGEMENT

PERMA is an acronym that stands for Positive emotions, Engagement, Relationships, Meaning, and Achievement—all of which combined lead to well-being. Here's an explanation of Engagement: *www.thepositivepsychologypeople.com/perma-e-is -for-engagement/*

Here's Seligman talking about PERMA. He's speaking to psychology students, so younger listeners might find this a bit slow going: *www.youtube.com/watch?v=iK6K_N2qe9Y*

Read for pleasure

Science shows there are many benefits to reading for pleasure. A daily or regular dose of a book you really enjoy can bring you better self-esteem, stronger empathy skills, greater knowledge and vocabulary, better sleep, success at school, fewer problems with stress, and generally an improved state of well-being.

So, if you love reading or if you liked it when you were younger but now feel you're too busy, or if you sometimes feel you should be working instead of reading for pleasure, take this as permission to do what you love: read! Curl up in a comfortable place, and keep the other members of your household out: this is your time. And don't let anyone tell you this is a waste of time: tell them about the science that shows it's benefiting you, not wasting time.

I invented a word for this: "readaxation." Readaxation means deliberately reading to relax. It works! You can try the activity on the next page, if you like.

★ A readaxation diary

First, read these statements and score 0–4 depending on how much you agree. Write the scores in your notebook. If you don't agree at all, score 0; if you strongly agree, score 4. Think carefully about your answers.

★ "It is usually easy for me to find a book I'll enjoy."

★ "Ideally, I would like to read for pleasure every day if possible."

★ "It is easy for me to make time for reading."

★ "Often when I read, I get carried away and involved in the story."

Now, each day for seven days, follow these steps:

★ Find a time when you won't be disturbed for about half an hour and take out a book you *want* to read. Find a comfortable place to read. (The best time is before bed.)

★ In your notebook, record your stress levels before you start reading, on a scale of 0–4. Think about symptoms such as a racing heart, shallow breathing, feeling anxious or tense.

★ Then read for about half an hour, letting yourself be carried away by the book.

★ Note your stress levels after you finish reading, again scoring 0–4.

If you didn't read on one day, don't record that day. Stop when you have seven days of records.

At the end of the week, ask yourself these questions:

★ Did reading an enjoyable book help me relax?

★ Do I think reading for pleasure might help lots of people feel better and be healthier?

★ Am I going to carry on doing it?!

(In **Resources** on page 195, you'll find a link to where you can download a readaxation diary. Your teacher or school librarian may also be interested.)

What should you read?

Whatever you want! Whatever you enjoy.
This is not a competition or an attempt to
"improve your mind" (though it will!). If you love fiction, read
fiction; if you prefer factual books, choose those; if graphic
novels are your taste, dive into them.

Sometimes an adult might comment that you've read the
same book many times and ask, "Can't you choose a more
challenging one?" But this is reading for pleasure, not reading
for challenge and improvement. Sometimes you might want to
read a more "challenging" book, but at the moment you want
to read this one. This is not the time for judgment. Adults don't
like to be judged on their reading choices, either.

Another thing adults might say is that a certain book is
"unsuitable" and might harm you. Very occasionally that
might be true. For example, if you have a mental illness, such
as anorexia nervosa, anxiety disorder, or depression, reading
certain books might make you feel worse. If you have any of
these or similar conditions, take advice on your reading choices
from an authority.

Sometimes adults want to protect teens from tough or
dark topics. This is quite understandable, but it's my strong
opinion—and I'm not alone among reading experts in thinking
this—that for most young people, reading about dark or
frightening topics in a book aimed at their age group is
the *safest* place to explore these things. It's better than the
Internet, where there is no control over the content. Stories
(true and made-up) are great ways to process worries and
grow our resilience and empathy.

If a book is going to be too dark for you, you will probably
know this before anything bad has happened and you'll be
able to put the book down. People do that all the time. I do.
So, read what interests you and be aware of how it affects
your mood.

Why is reading for pleasure so good?

There are two main reasons. First, it occupies many areas of the brain and requires concentration, so it is easy to "engage" deeply. Second, it allows us to forget our worries for a while. After all, you can't be fully involved in a book *and* worry at the same time.

What if you don't like reading?

That's OK. Not everyone does. And if you don't like it, I won't force you. But there are so many benefits that I want you to know them and see if you'd like to try again. Remember: you can read *anything*, either in print or on an e-book reader. It can be true or made-up; it can be about sports, heroes, crocodiles, baking, murderers, highwaymen, horses, cars; it can be set in India or Iceland, in the desert or underwater; it can feature characters of every color or background, from history or today; it can be sad or happy or funny or scary. It can have as many pictures in it as you want. It's all up to you.

What about audiobooks?

Excellent idea! Of course, it's not doing exactly the same thing in your brain (because any two different activities will have some different effects), but it's a perfectly valid way of relaxing and engaging with a book and its characters, events, and emotions. So, if you like listening instead of reading yourself, go for it. Lots of adults like this, too.

When should you do it?

Whenever you feel like it! I think the best time is before bed, after you've done everything to get yourself ready for sleep.

194

Most people find reading a great way to switch off the day and will start feeling sleepy very quickly. Some people find they get so into a book that they can't sleep, especially if the book is really exciting. If this happens to you, it's best to set a timer and limit your reading time to about forty-five minutes.

POSITIVE BOOST

Can you remember a story you loved when you were much younger? Could you find it now? Maybe you have younger siblings and love their books? Go and find a special favorite. Have fun reading it. Remember how you felt as a child. Just take five minutes with one of these lovely, inspiring books.

Resources

READING FOR PLEASURE

Science shows there are a lot of benefits to reading for pleasure. The 2015 UK Reading Agency report gathered the research: *readingagency .org.uk/news/media/reading-for-pleasure-builds-empathy-and -improves-well-being-research-from-the-reading-agency-finds.html*

My website has lots of links to research and resources, including a readaxation diary to monitor the stress-relieving effects of reading before bed. Go to *www.nicolamorgan.com* and see the Reading Brain section, or enter "readaxation" in the search box.

Just think

It's something many people don't do anymore: just spending time thinking. Any bits of spare time we have, we seem to fill with entertainment, or connecting with other people online, or getting information or messages from our phones or other devices. All those things are good, but because so many of us (including me!) have a phone with us pretty much all the time, it's so easy just to pick it up instead of spending time in our own heads.

Why might that matter? What's the problem if your mind and time are filled with all that lovely online activity and there's no time to think freely? (This applies to all age groups, by the way, even though I'm saying "your.")

I think it matters for several reasons.

✳ It's mentally exhausting. All these activities use brain energy. Just as you have to rest your body sometimes, you also have to rest your brain. Otherwise it won't work as well.

✳ The messages on smartphones or computers are often stressful. If you didn't get enough "likes" on a post or if someone else's selfie looks so much more gorgeous than yours or someone says something slightly (or very) undermining, it will dampen your mood. If that happens too much, it's not healthy.

✳ Thinking is important and creative and exciting!

Let's consider that last one. Creative people say that their best ideas don't usually come when they're staring at a computer screen, but when they're taking a walk, or on a bus or train, or in the shower or bath, or doing nothing at all. Ask any writer, artist, engineer, designer, or computer-game creator.

And it's not just people who obviously need creative thinking time. It applies to people who start businesses, planning to make their dreams come true. Teachers, thinking about a problem with a class. Filmmakers, constructing their next project. Parents, wondering how to help their children feel more confident at school or planning a weekend activity for everyone to enjoy. Scientists and psychologists, grappling with a new idea. Gardeners, deciding when to sow seeds for the best crop. Managers, trying to figure out how to make their staff function better.

It's not just for work, either. We all need time to think about ourselves and our dreams, problems, strengths, and ideas. What we want from life and how to get it, who our friends are, how to help a friend in need, and how to thank a friend for something they've done.

There's even research to suggest that deliberate daydreaming time helps creative thinking and forward-planning. Scientists believe that it's when we're *not* actively thinking about something that our mind can be doing its best work. I'm not saying you should spend all day daydreaming, especially in class, though! This research is about *deliberately* letting your thoughts drift every now and then, not letting anyone else (or a smartphone) distract you, but letting your mind wander for a while. Then come back to the task at hand and find that your thinking is clearer. This is particularly useful when you've been struggling with something you're trying to understand or work out: if you spend maybe twenty minutes of real effort and then go for a short walk to a store or lie in the backyard for a while, or relax on your bed, maybe listening to music but not focusing on anything in particular, you'll often find that when you go back to what you originally struggled with, you can do it. Our minds do a lot of work when we aren't trying! But we have to give ourselves the mental space for that to happen.

The world needs thinkers, and thinkers need thinking time!

Ideas

✻ Next time you're traveling anywhere, leave your phone hidden away. Just don't take it out. Look out the window and let your mind free-associate.

✻ Is there something you want to think about or need to plan? A school project or play, something you want to do with your friends? Set some time aside for it. Put your phone away and switch the Internet off.

✻ Go for a walk on your own. (Be safe.) Focus on what you can see and hear around you.

✻ Take a bath, with no book, magazine, or phone to distract you.

✻ If you find it difficult or even scary just letting your mind freewheel, try some simple meditation or mindfulness techniques. Try the relaxation technique on the following page.

✻ Help settle your mind with a simple activity that doesn't require much thought: weeding the garden, doodling, knitting (if you're good at it), playing with a stress ball, making a collage from magazines, listening to music. All these things take up a little bit of brain bandwidth, but not too much. You can still think while doing them.

This kind of thinking time really can't be done with anyone else, so it's especially important for quieter or introverted people, who need time on their own. Some kind people might ask if you're OK, so just say: "Definitely, but I'm thinking and I need peace and quiet for that."

Don't be afraid of "doing nothing." It's really good for you (sometimes)!

POSITIVE BOOST

Sit or lie somewhere really comfortable, where you won't be disturbed. Breathe in deeply through your nose and out more slowly through your mouth. Close your eyes. Focus on your toes and feet. Tense those muscles, and then relax. Now move on to your legs and do the same. Do this tensing and relaxing for each part of your body, working your way up to your head.

Think of the tension floating away through the top of your head. Think about each muscle in your face and jaw. Continue breathing in a relaxed way. Feel your muscles get heavier and softer. Stay like this for as long as you want. When you're ready, open your eyes and get up slowly.

POSITIVELY YOU · A POSITIVE ATTITUDE · POSITIVELY HEALTHY · POSITIVELY BRAINY · POSITIVE ABOUT PEOPLE · A POSITIVE MOOD

Resources

<u>THINKING</u>

Freedom to Think: *http://freedomtothinksite.tumblr.com/about*

Deliberate daydreaming may help creative thinking and forward-planning: *www.telegraph.co.uk/news/2016/05/23/daydreaming-can-boost-your-daily-productivity--research-suggests/*

The *Atlantic*, with references to various studies about the need for young people to have daydreaming and thinking time: *www.theatlantic.com/education/archive/2013/10/teach-kids-to-daydream/280615/*

Some successful people and their attitude to thinking time; aimed at adults, but these same things should apply to you: *www.inc.com/empact/why-successful-people-spend-10-hours-a-week-just-thinking.html*

POSITIVE BOOST

What would you like as a reward for learning so much? Half an hour lying in the park? Movies with friends? A day at the beach? Cake or ice cream, just for a treat? Whatever it is, as long as you're allowed, go for it. You deserve it!

Focus on the positive

This book is all about focusing on the positives, and this section is about having a positive mood, but sometimes bad things happen, even when we do everything right.

When that happens, it's completely natural to feel really negative, whether sad, shocked, angry, scared, guilty, regretful, confused, or whatever. But after a while we have to start to pick ourselves up. That's when tricks to focus on the positives come in handy.

Sometimes, nothing in particular has happened, but we still feel a bit low. It's often too easy to think about the bad stuff when, in fact, there are lots of good things in our lives.

When something difficult happens, we can't control how we feel about it right away, because emotions just happen, rather than being things we decide about. Later, however, we *can* begin to control how we feel. In fact, that's part of well-being—being able to decide that we're going to feel better and taking steps to make that happen. Sometimes we might need extra help, and that's when you should see a doctor. Also, of course, really major bad things take longer to recover from.

But for most people, most of the time, there are things we can do to help us focus on positives rather than negatives.

Ideas

✳ Make sure you have something to look forward to. What is it? A vacation? Your birthday? The holidays? What do you hope it will be like? Or pick something closer in time: plan a trip to the movies; arrange to meet a good friend. Something nice over the weekend can make the whole week feel better.

✳ What went well? Don't forget to say what character strengths you used.

✳ Positive daydreaming. You can be as creative as you like, and no one will ever know what you're daydreaming about. It could have all your heroes in it; you could have loads of money and be thinking about how to spend it; you could win prizes and achieve your heart's desire. Or you could be lying on a perfect beach, at peace, with just the sound of lapping waves. It's just a daydream, and you can control it.

✳ In your notebook, jot down three good things about your life; three goals you have for next week; three people who are on your side; three positive things about being a teen.

Summing up

You might have thought mood was something you can't control, that you just wake up in a good or bad mood. Certainly, outside events affect mood, and sometimes it's not easy to be happy when difficult thoughts are spinning around.

But I hope you see now that there are quite simple things you can do to improve your mood. This section has given you a lot of practical suggestions to help you manage your well-being, beginning with knowing how to identify your own stress symptoms, then using your environment, music, laughter, engaging hobbies, reading, or just thinking and daydreaming for a while to give yourself a break from our busy world.

You mood is a bit like making a snowball: build it up and it gets bigger. So make sure you go with your good moods, adding positive things to them, and stomp on your bad moods so they don't have a chance to snowball.

★ The FLOURISH test again

Remember how you did the FLOURISH test near the start of the book? How about doing it again, as long as you haven't read the whole book in the same day?! If you have, do it again this time tomorrow. Did you score better the second time?

Finally...

So, there you have it: everything I can think of to keep you positively teen!

You might have started this book because you were excited about being a teenager or just plain curious about what might lie ahead. Being curious is a really good reason to read a book like this because information and understanding are so empowering. Or you might have had some anxiety and were looking for reassurance—I certainly hope *Positively Teen* is full of it. You might already have started noticing that your thoughts and feelings weren't behaving quite the same way they did a couple of years ago, and you wanted to know how normal that is. Answer: totally!

I hope the main thing you've discovered is that you can control far, far more than you thought possible. You've learned a lot of strategies to use throughout your life, starting with these exciting, dramatic, changing teen years. If things go wrong, you can be resilient, pick yourself up, grow stronger, and move forward. You have a huge toolbox to control physical and mental well-being and be positive about your life, your potential, yourself. Many of these are the same tools adults should know but often don't: maybe you can share this knowledge with your parents and teachers.

You have the power to make yourself FLOURISH, throughout your life. Use your powers well!

Be truly, positively teen!

adolescence—literally "becoming adult"; the stage of development between child and adult.

adrenaline—a chemical (**hormone**) produced in the body to make us super alert, strong, and ready for action, especially when we are scared or excited.

aerobic exercise—also called "cardio," this is light to moderate exercise that we can keep going for some time, unlike sprinting or weight lifting, which we can only do briefly.

body mass index—a healthy weight must relate to our *height, age, and sex*. A BMI chart shows the healthy range for each of us.

calories—measurements of the energy that a particular portion of food would provide. If we don't eat enough calories, we lack energy, our brain works less well, and we may be unhealthily thin.

cortisol—along with adrenaline, a **hormone** the body produces in response to stress, making us alert and ready for action in the face of threat or need to perform super well.

diabetes—there are two main types of diabetes, involving failure to produce or process insulin, which regulates blood sugar, or **glucose**. In Type 1, which usually begins in childhood, patients need daily injections and must monitor blood sugar very carefully. Type 2 is much more common and is diet related. It is usually managed through diet and weight control. Diabetes is a growing problem in countries where people eat too much sugar.

diuretic—anything that makes the body produce more urine.

dopamine—an extremely important brain chemical (neurotransmitter) that helps **neurons** send messages around the body. It's vital for learning and memory, mood, pleasure and excitement, sleep, and many other human behaviors.

eczema—a condition where patches of skin become extremely dry and itchy. It can be soothed with creams and by avoiding things that trigger it, which differ between sufferers.

endorphins—**hormones** produced in the brain that make us feel less pain.

genes—the bits of "code" that we inherit from our biological parents and that affect many aspects of how we look, grow, and behave. Genes are "switched on or off" by the environment or things that happen to us, so it's more complicated than simply inheriting them. Genes are not responsible for *everything* about us, but they are fascinating and important.

glucose—a simple sugar that our body processes, using the **hormone** insulin, and carries in the blood to use as energy. People with **diabetes** have to test the glucose level in their blood often.

heart rate—how many times the heart beats per minute. When we are sitting still and feeling calm, our heart beats more slowly than when we are exercising or stressed. People who are in good shape tend to have a slower "resting" heart rate than others. Healthy heart rate varies according to age.

hormones—chemicals produced in the body that regulate everything our bodies do. The sex hormones, for example—testosterone, androstenedione, estrogen, and progesterone—make the bodily changes that turn us into a fully developed adult of whichever sex. There are hormones to control appetite, sleep, growth, mood, digestion, and every process our body needs to be healthy. There's even one—oxytocin—that makes you feel love or desire!

neuron—also called a "nerve cell," a cell in the brain and spinal cord that sends messages to the rest of the body. We are born with around one hundred billion neurons, and later we lose many of these as part of natural, healthy pruning. We don't need them all! Our skills and abilities come from how well our neurons connect into pathways, not how many neurons we have. Every time we practice anything, we grow and strengthen these pathways.

nutrients—all the parts of food that help nourish us, including vitamins, proteins, and minerals. Each nutrient has a special job, so it's important to eat a wide range of foods. The word "nutritious" comes from the same word.

prefrontal cortex—the area of the brain at the very front, more developed in humans than other animals. It's often called the "control center" because we use it for things such as controlling actions and thoughts, making good decisions, working things out, making moral judgments, and understanding what might happen next. It's the last area of the brain to develop fully, which happens well into our twenties.

puberty—the stage when "secondary sex characteristics" begin to develop, with the biological function of making us able to reproduce. Young people (usually from about ages ten to eleven for girls and twelve for boys, though this varies a lot between individuals) will notice many changes in their bodies, with some starting earlier or later than others. Puberty is triggered by the sex **hormones**.

psychology—the study of behavior, why we do and feel the way we do. Early psychologists studied what went wrong and how to fix it, but psychology now also focuses on how to prevent problems by understanding how we all work.

social anxiety—anxiety in social situations is very common, and most people feel a bit nervous or shy when they are with people they don't know well. But social anxiety (also called social phobia) is a more extreme form of this, and occurs when a sufferer finds it really difficult or impossible to cope in social situations and becomes extremely stressed. There is better understanding of this now, and lots of help available.

species—in biology, a species is a group of animals similar enough to breed naturally together. Humans and gorillas are both "primates" (apes), but they are not the same species. The species name for humans is *Homo sapiens*. Barn owls and snowy owls are both owls, but they each come from a different species of owl; they don't breed together.

Index